I0488355

# MICHAEL NELSON

## Recent Drawings

# Recent Drawings

The following drawings were created between 2012 and 2016 in a small 5"x8" sketchbook on a train moving from Long Island to Manhattan. At the time I was working full time as a display artist for Urban Outfitters in Manhattan. This varied and creative job provided me a way to raise a family in the suburbs just outside of the city. My spare time was full of adult responsibilities as a home owner, father, and husband. Unable to commit serious time to making personal work, I began drawing on my morning commute. Departing Long Island at 4:50am, the quiet train provided me an hour to dedicate to drawing. These drawings began as a way to explore themes for future works, but as time moved on, the practice of standing and drawing became second nature and these notes became works in and of themselves. Presented here are some drawings that touch on symbolic themes that have bubbled up over the past years. Arranged by theme, some drawings shown together were created years apart. My intentions were basic - to communicate a thought, to bring something I was feeling to the surface and give it form, to wrestle with myself through this medium to better understand the world and my place in it. As for technique, these drawings were created discretely in a half open book, on a moving train full of sleepy commuters. They are small, lightly drawn, and created within an hour.

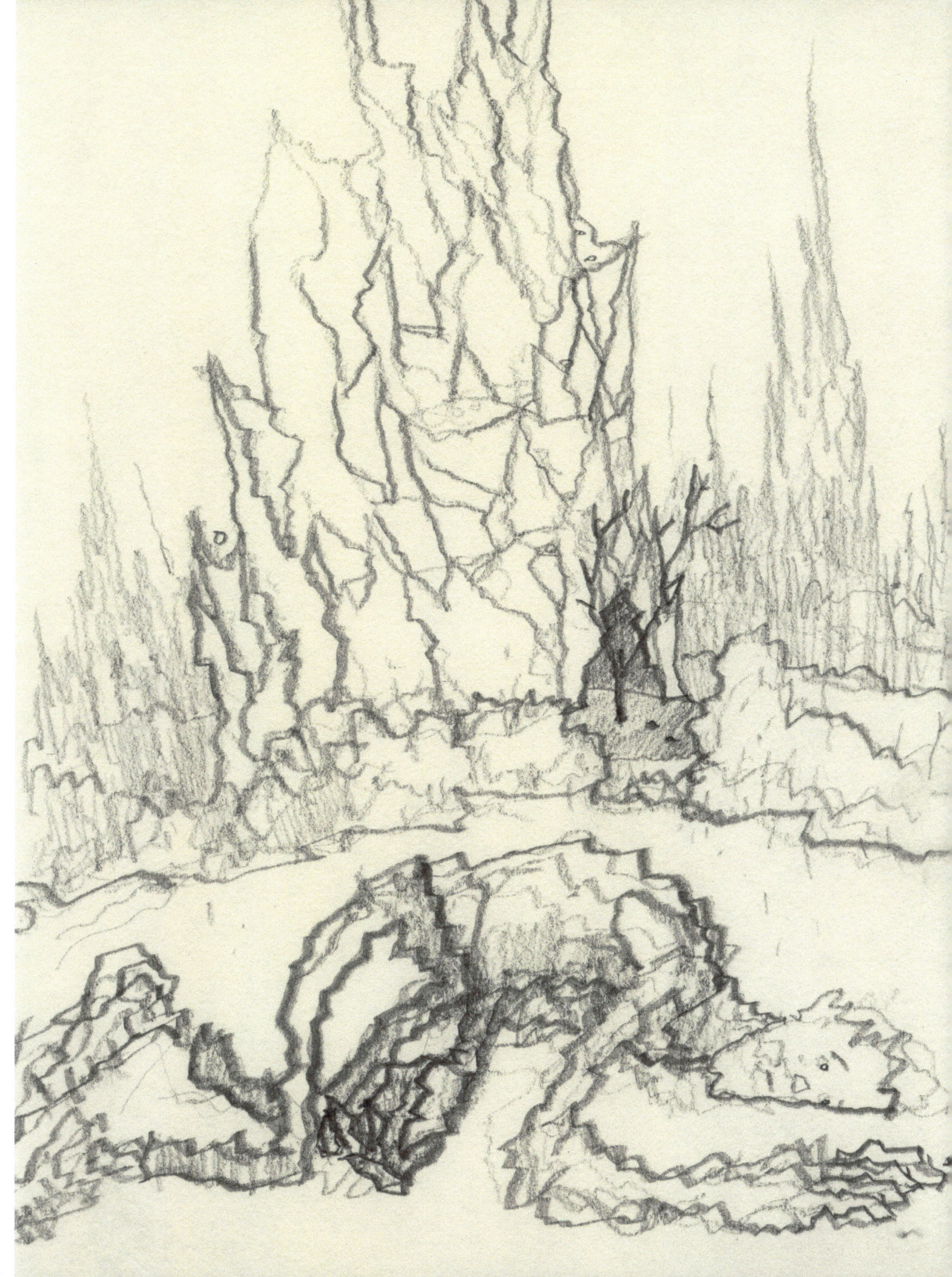

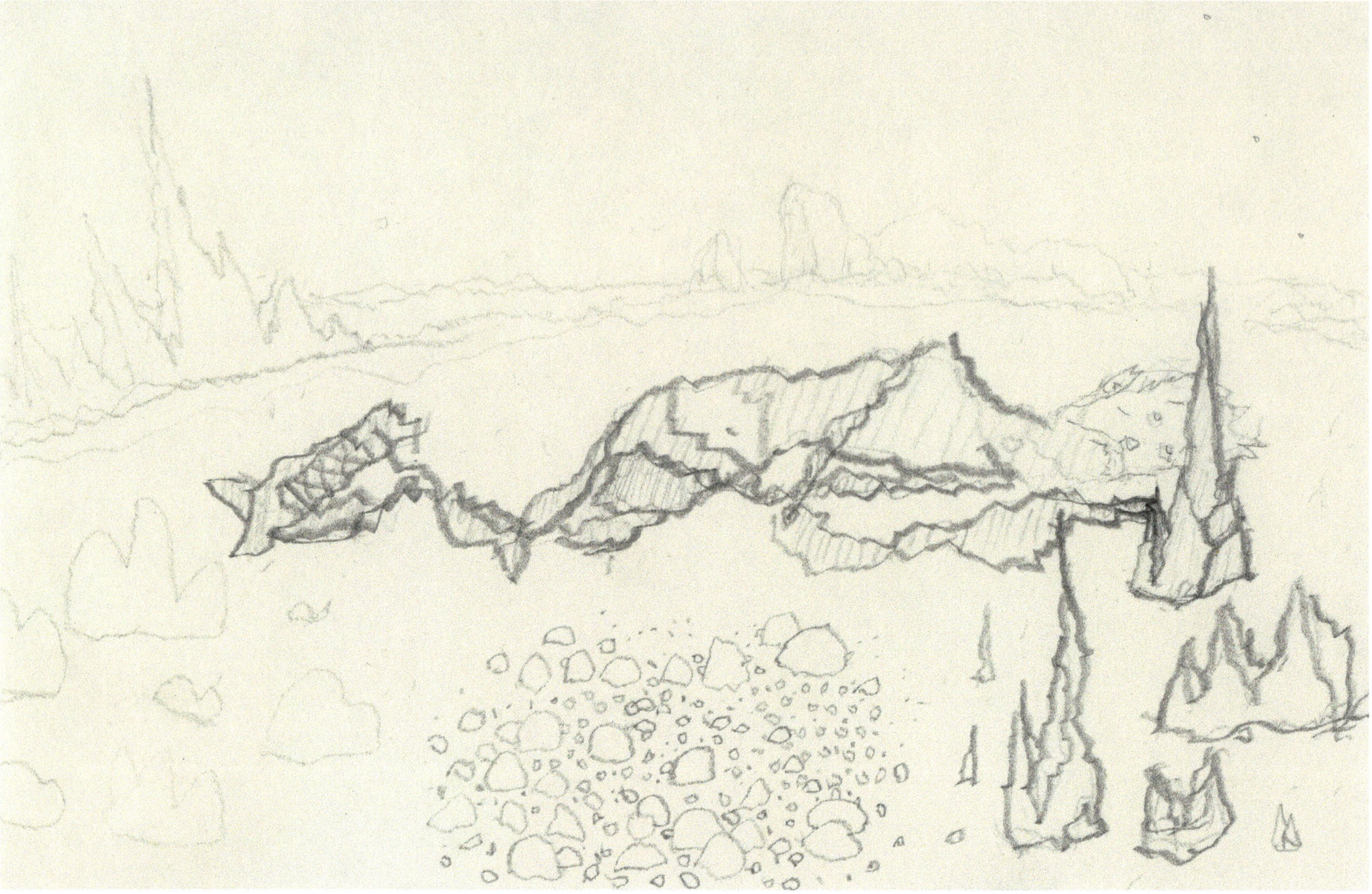

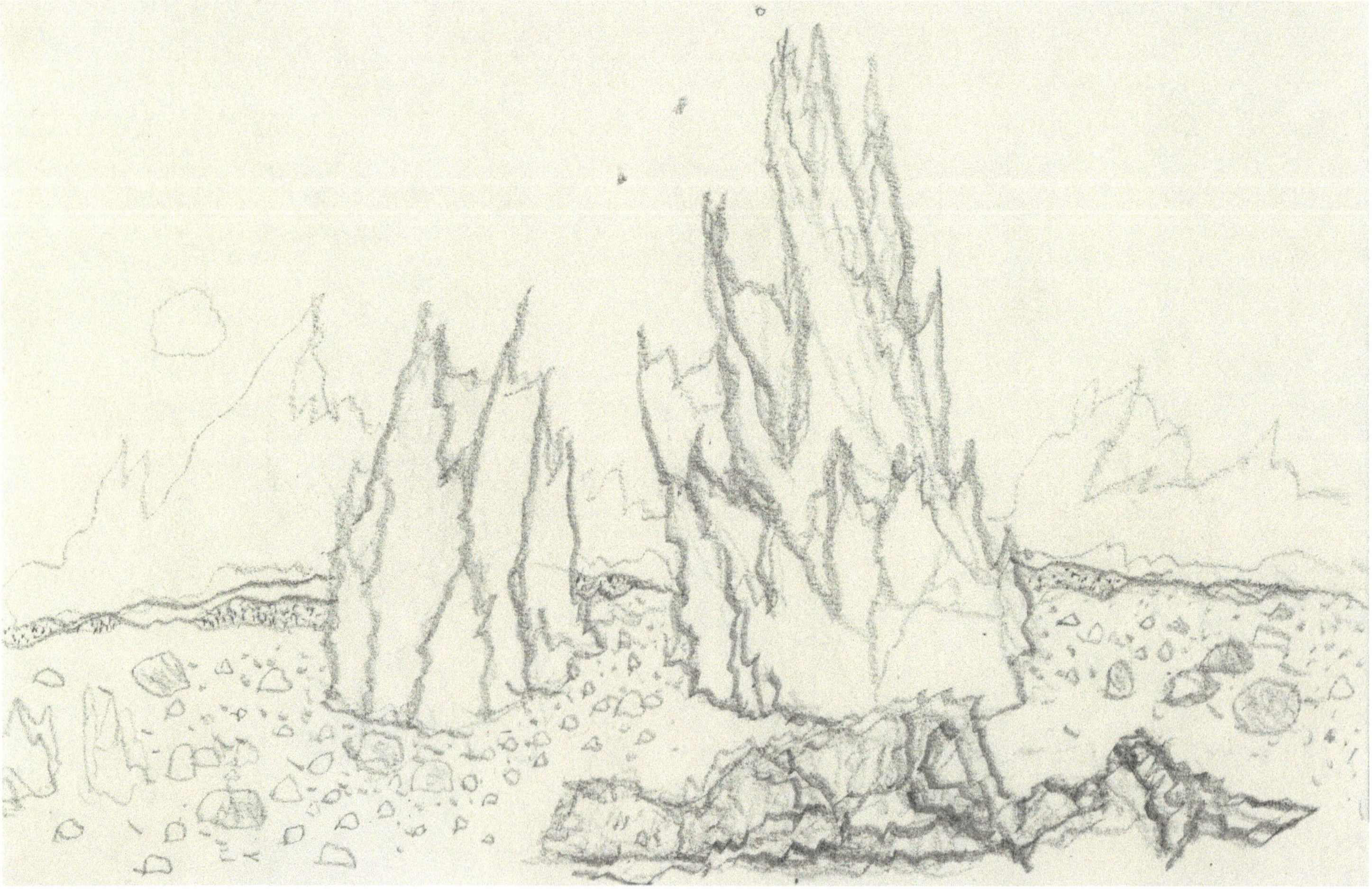

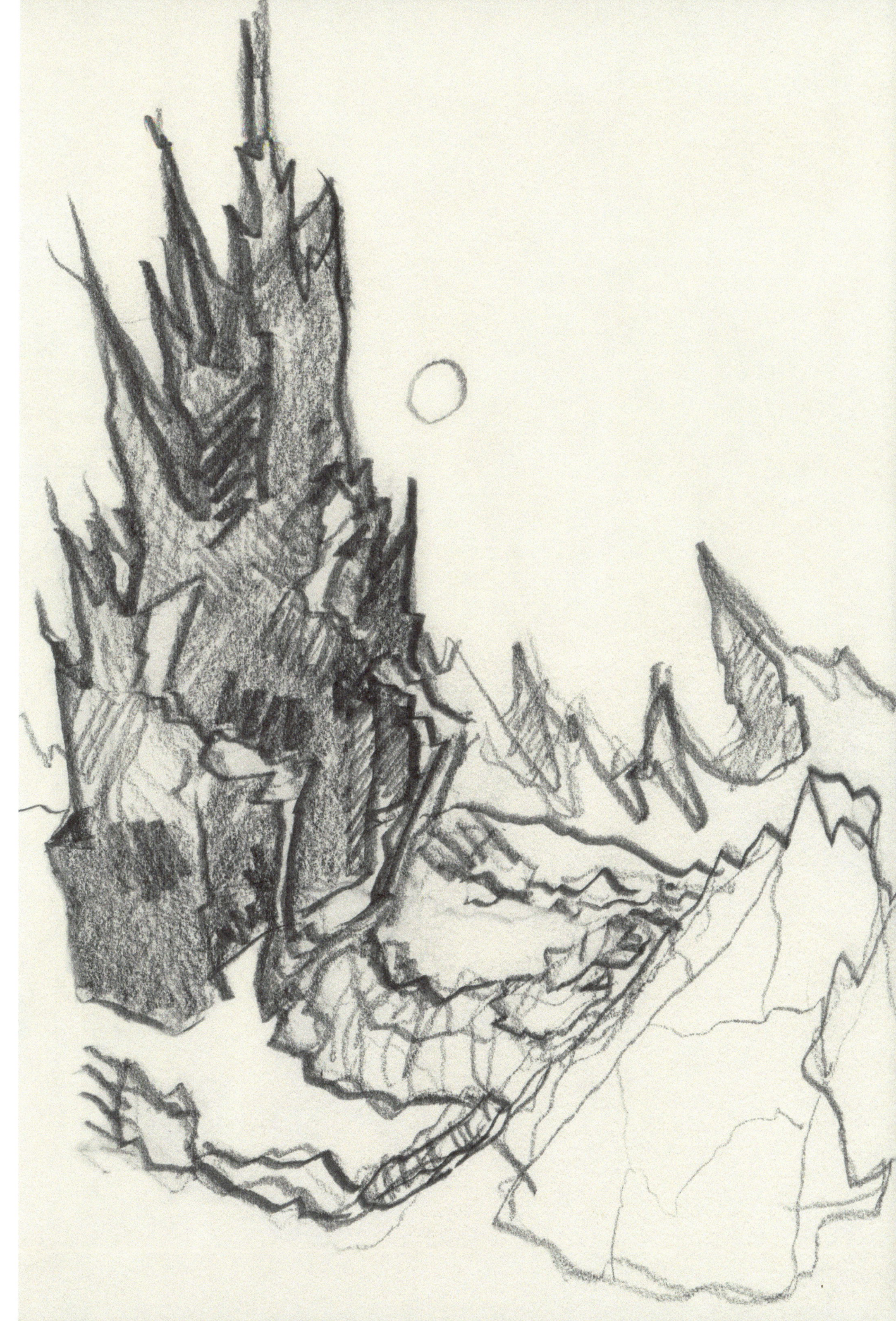

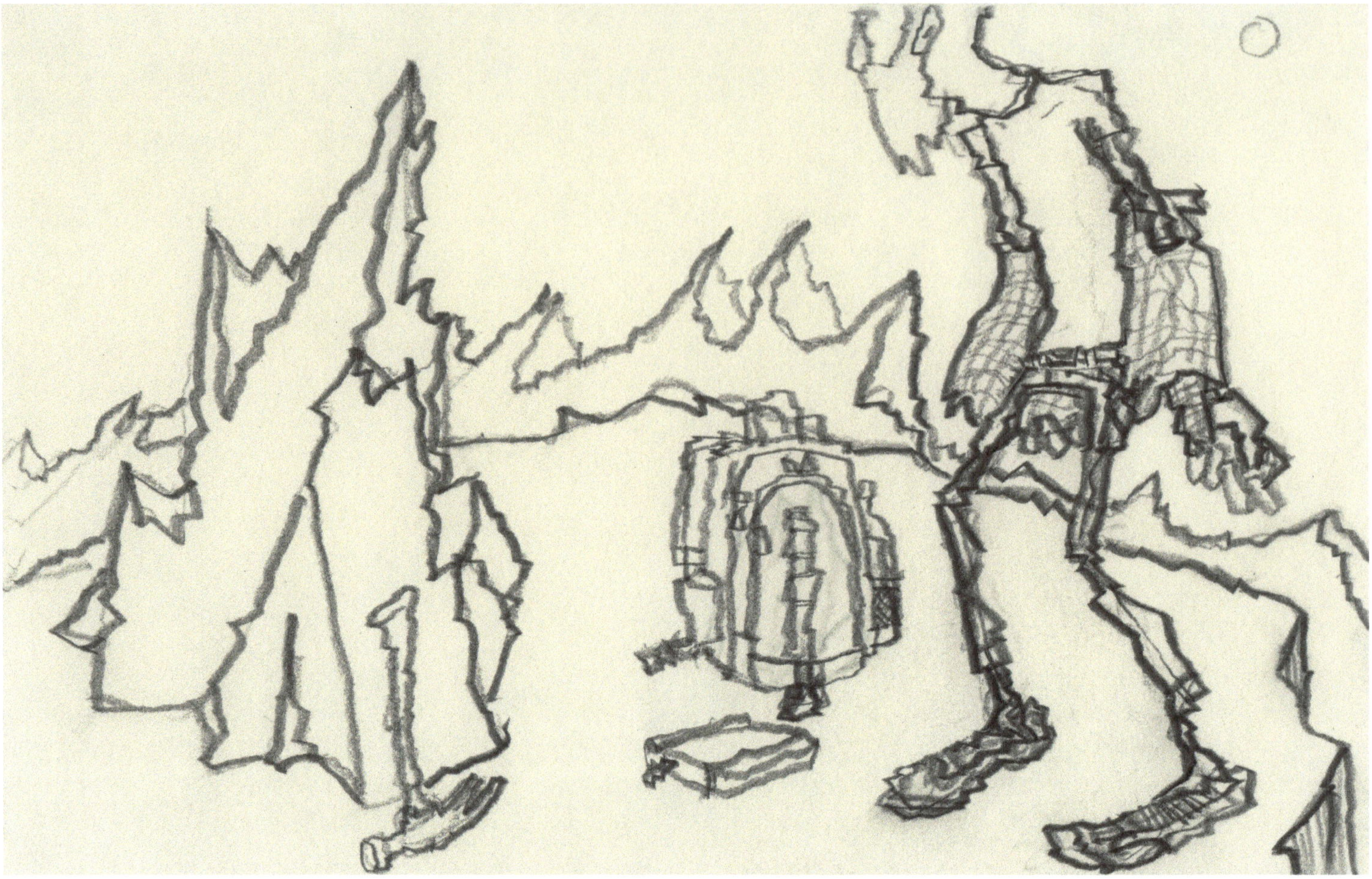

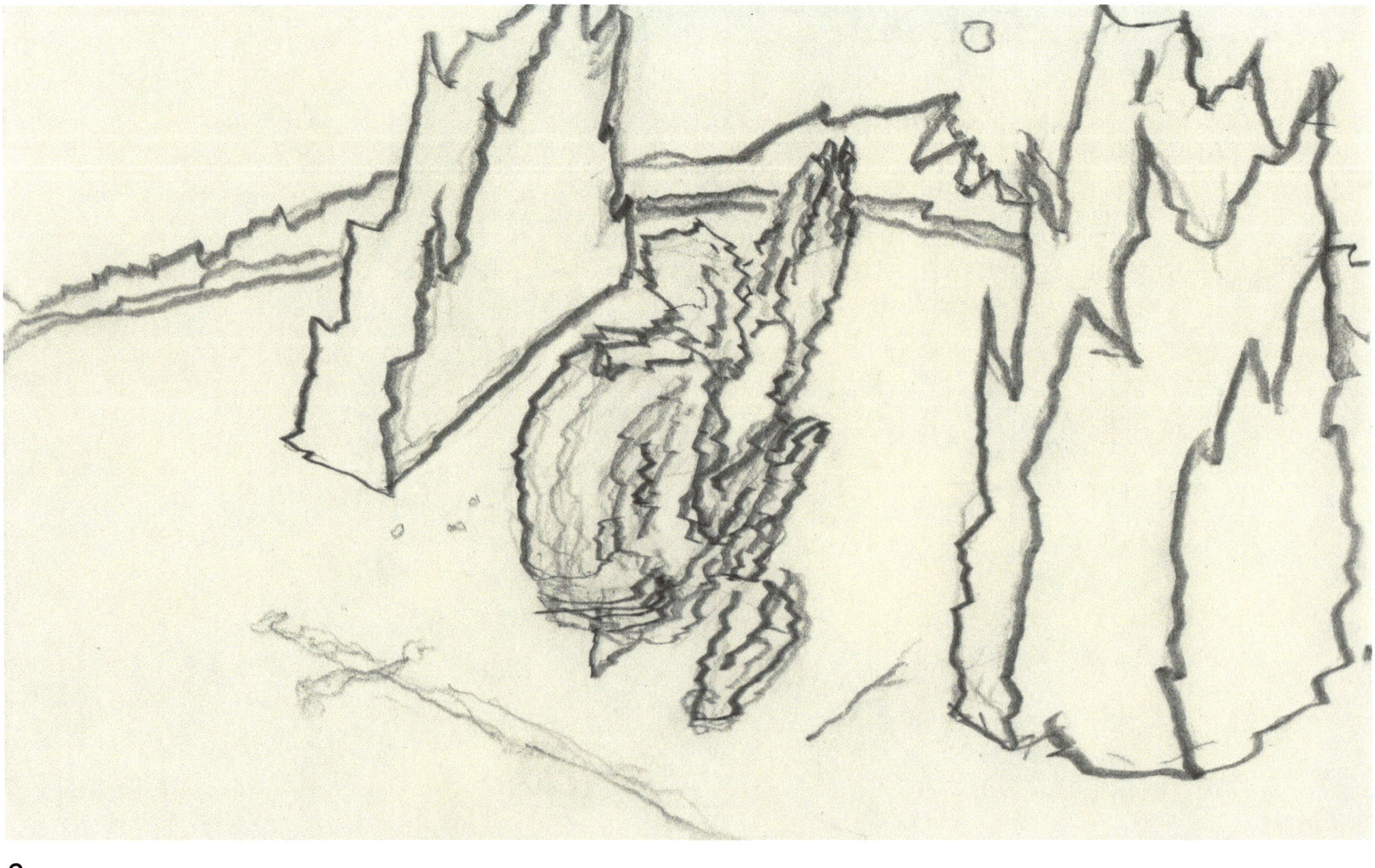

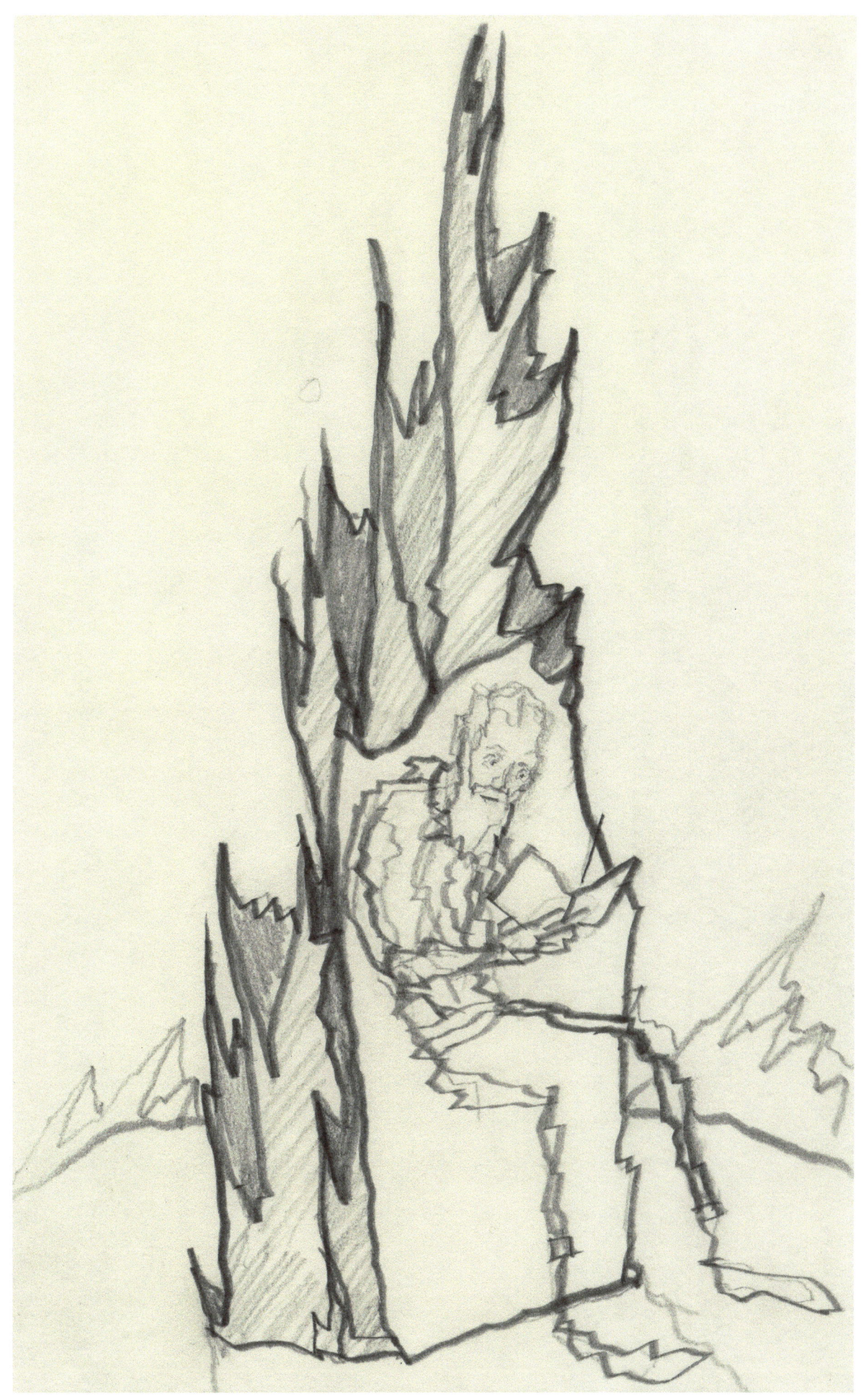

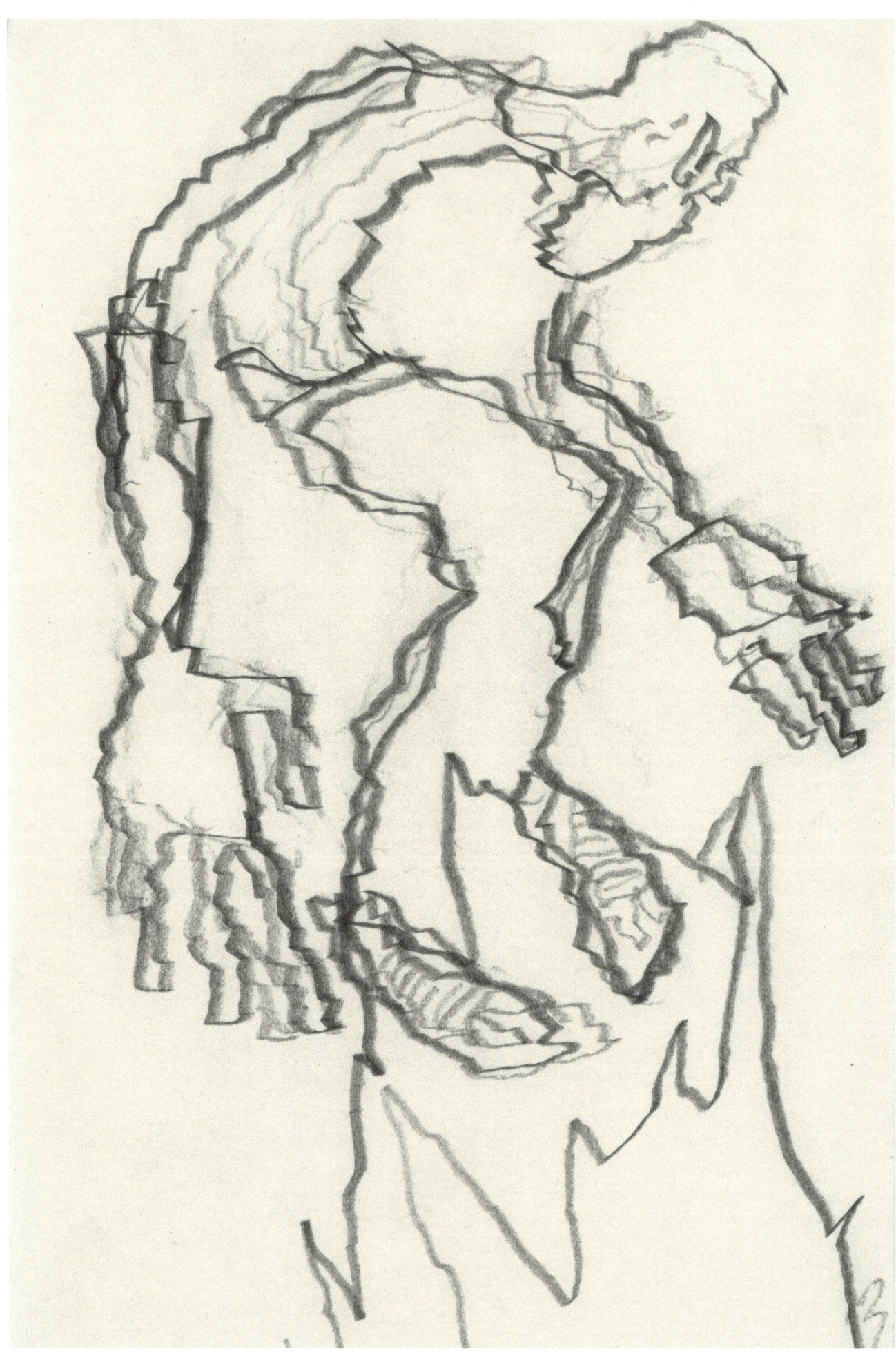

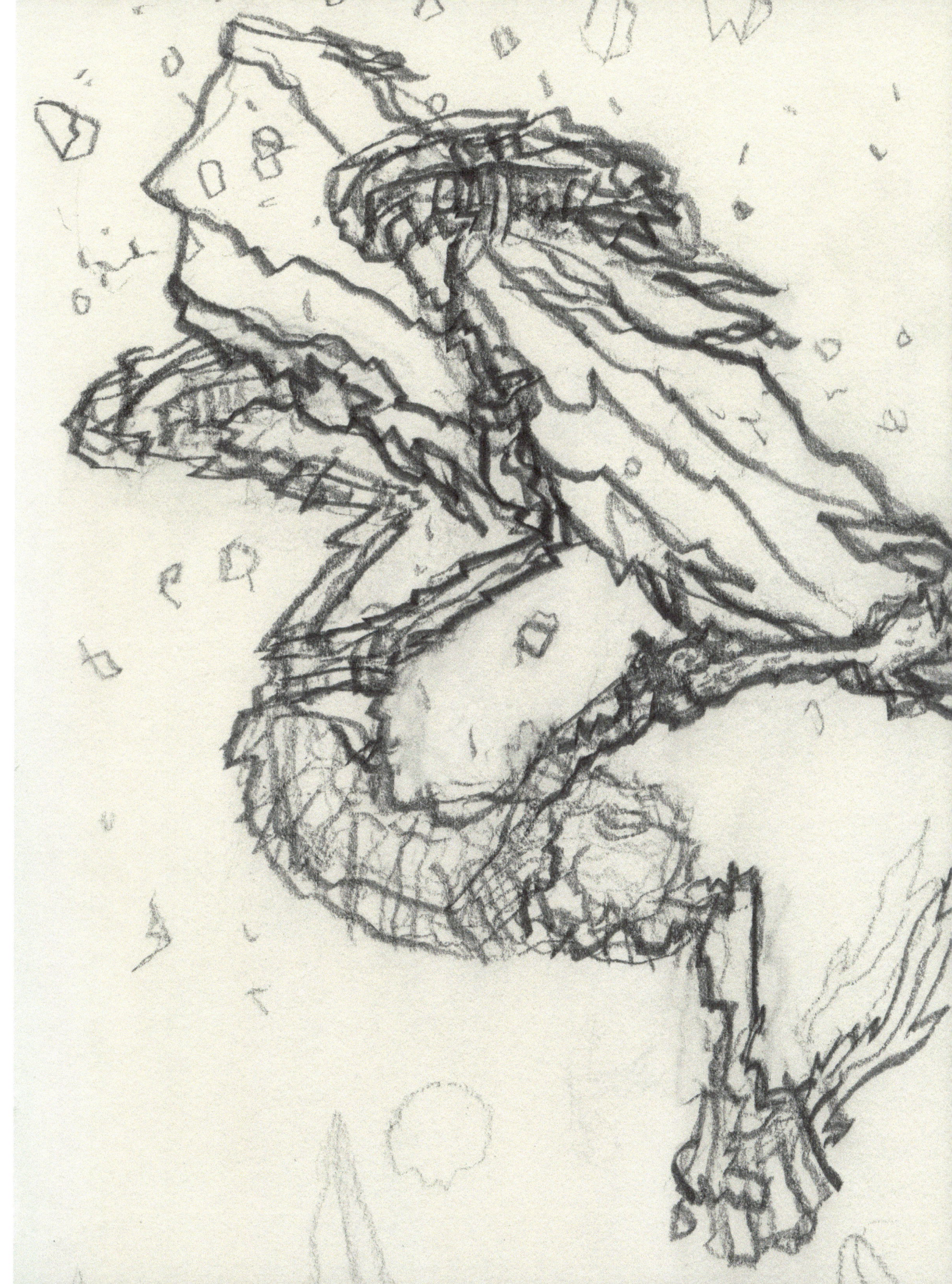

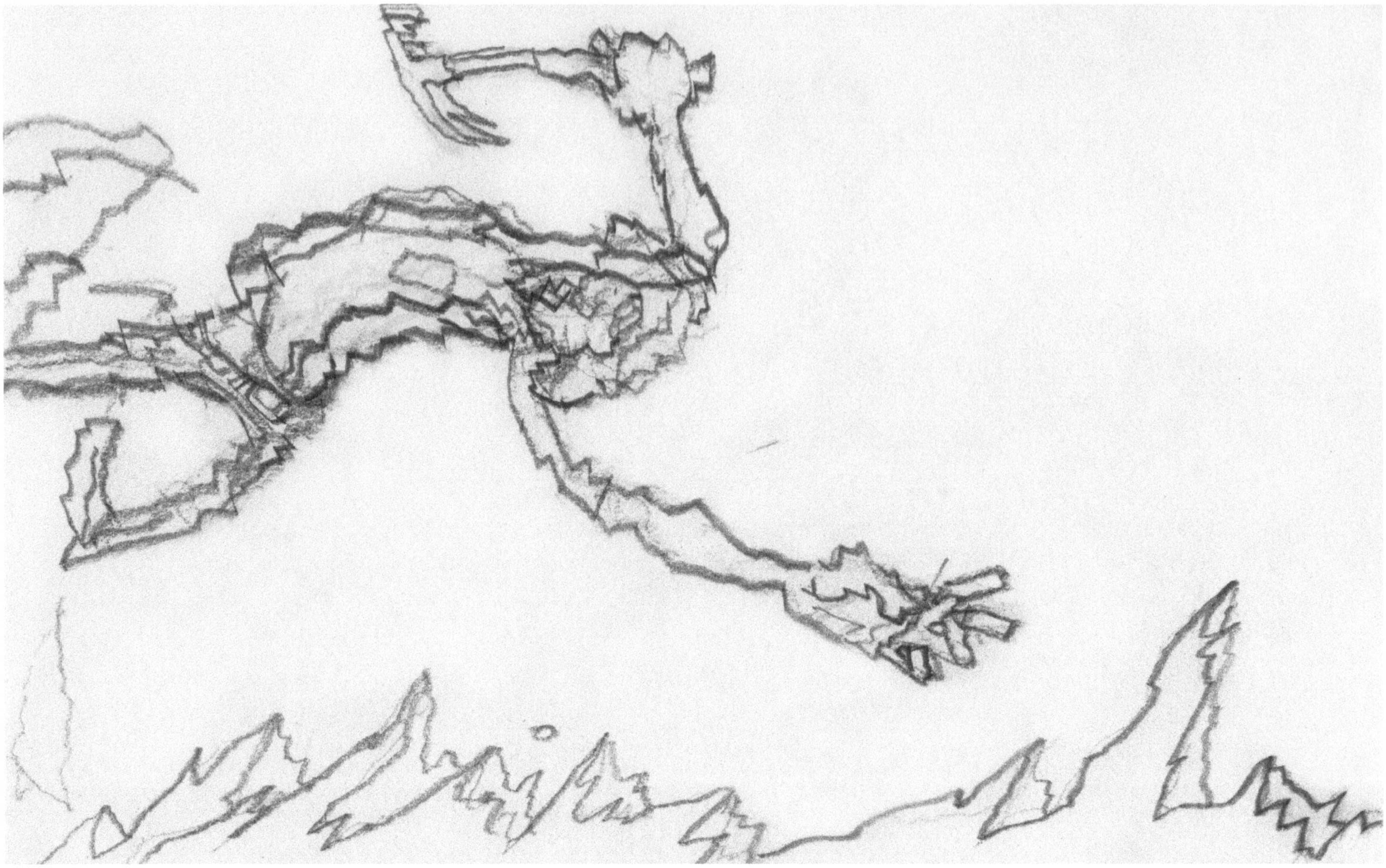

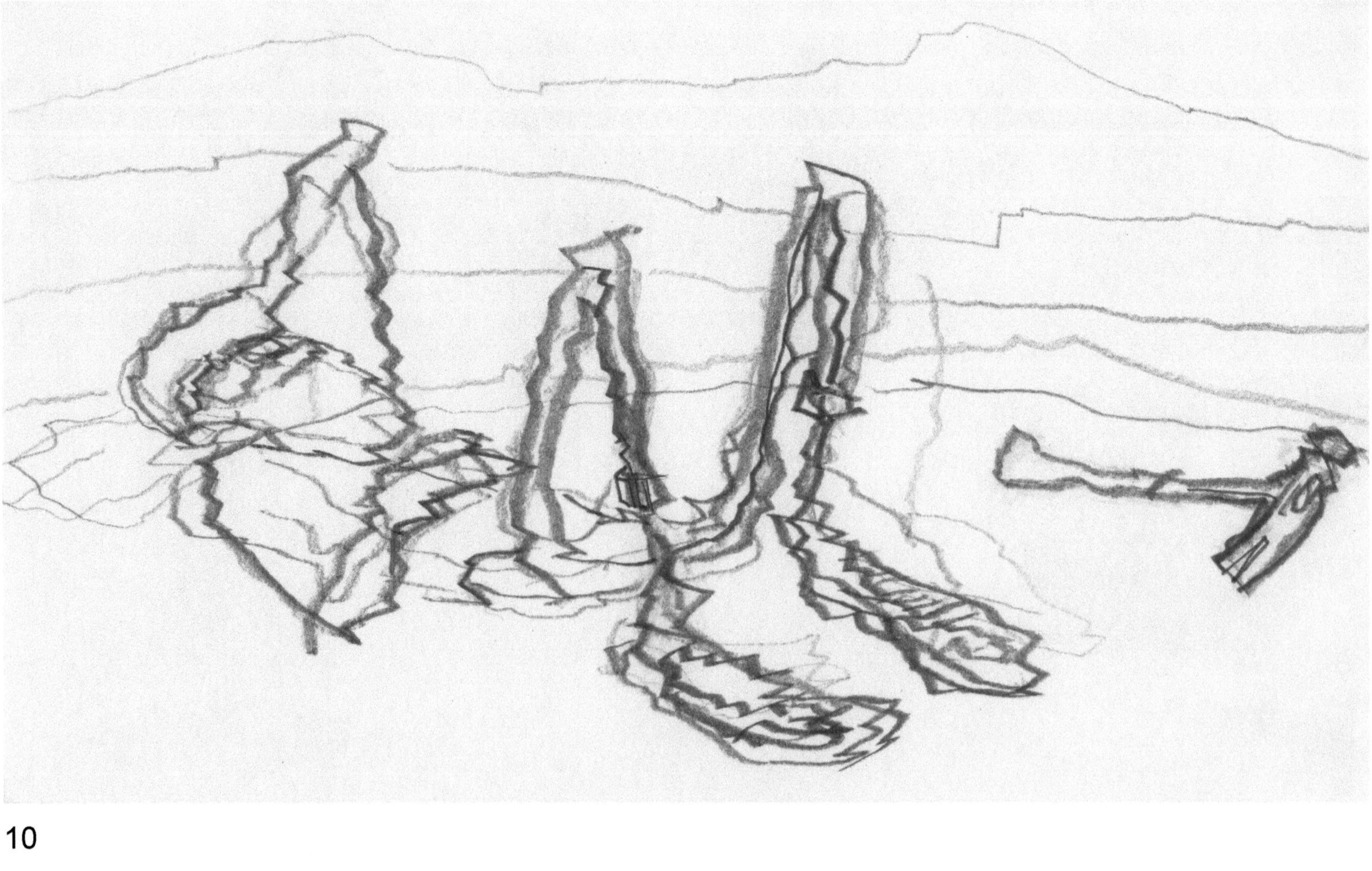

10

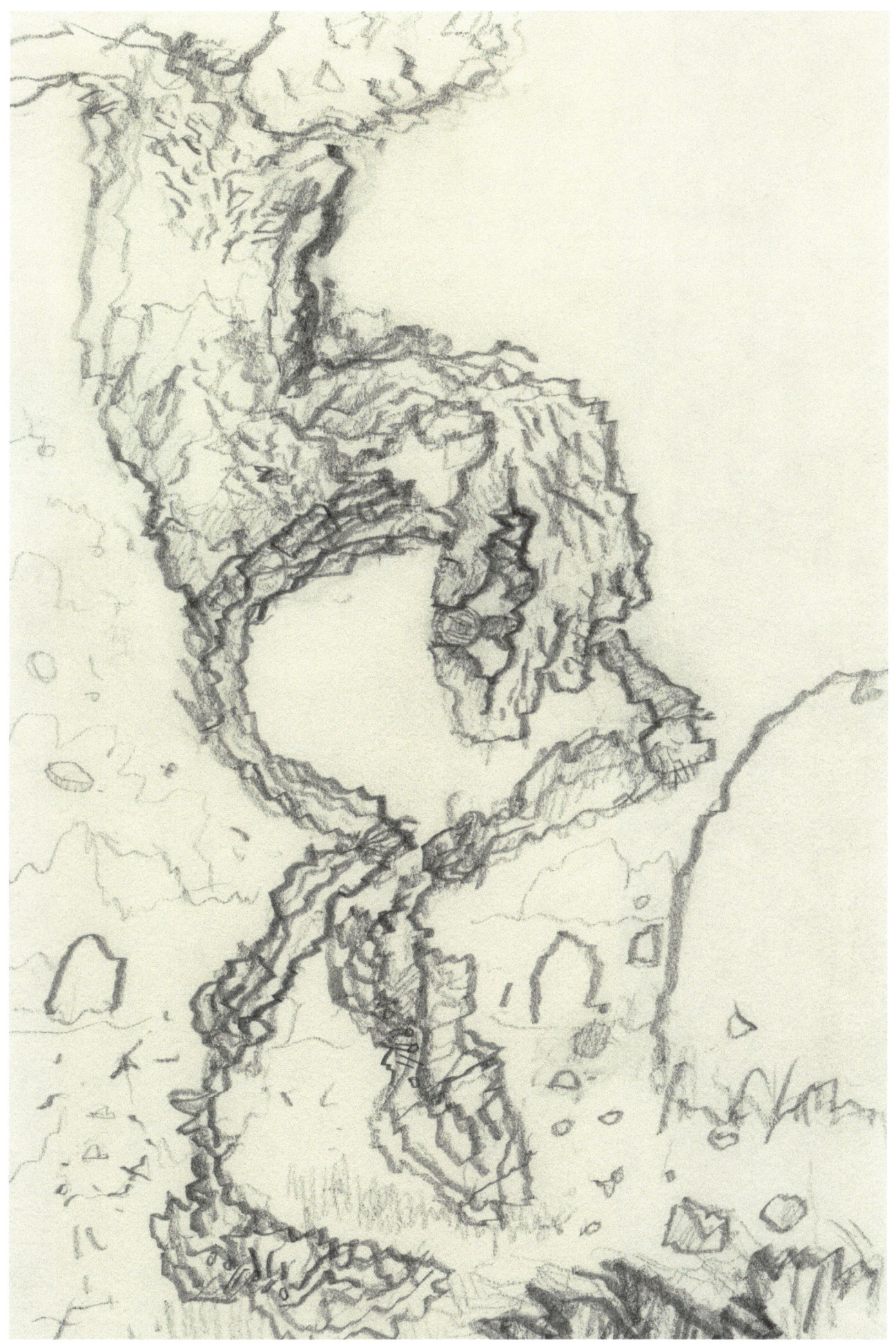

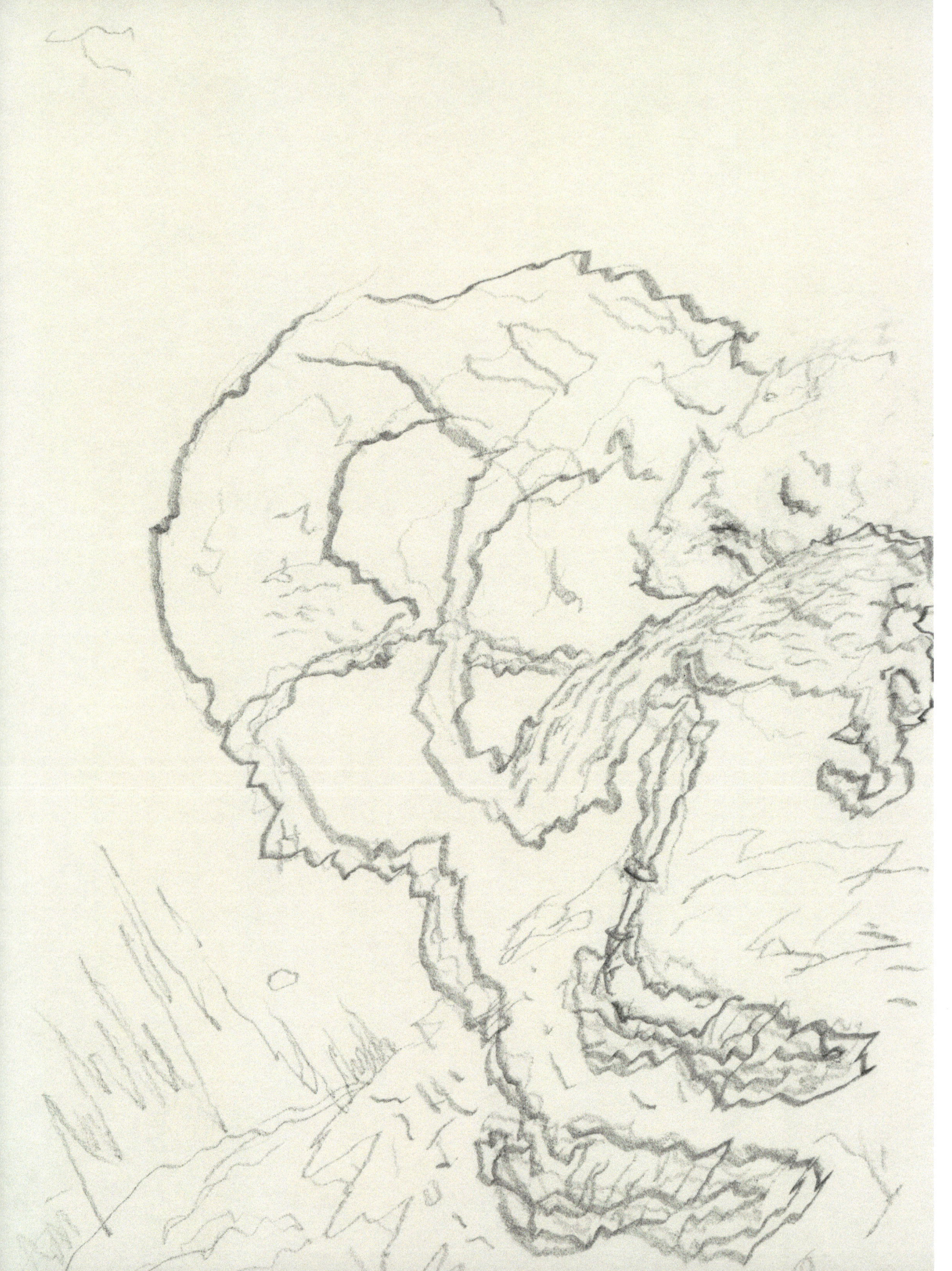

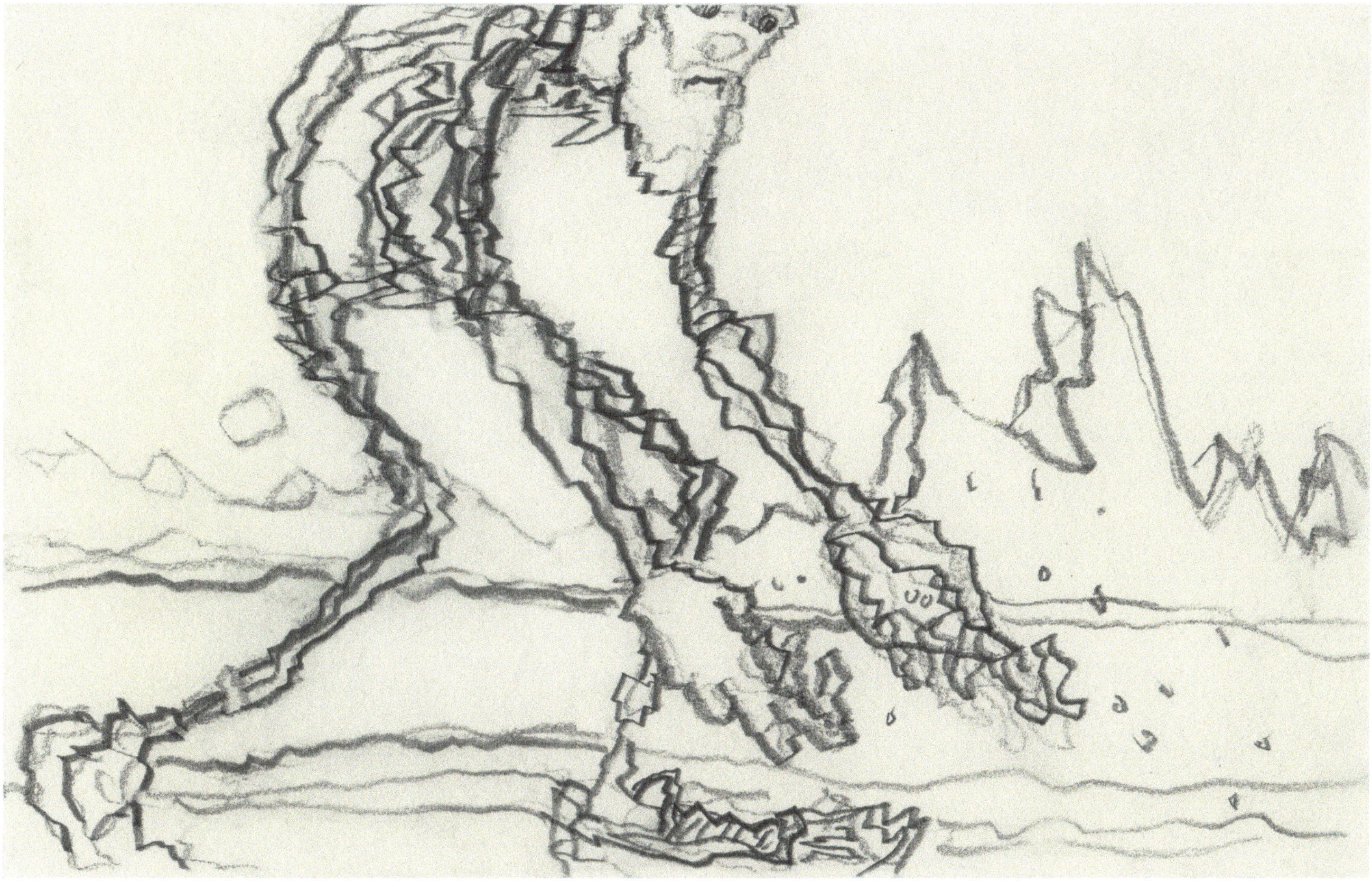

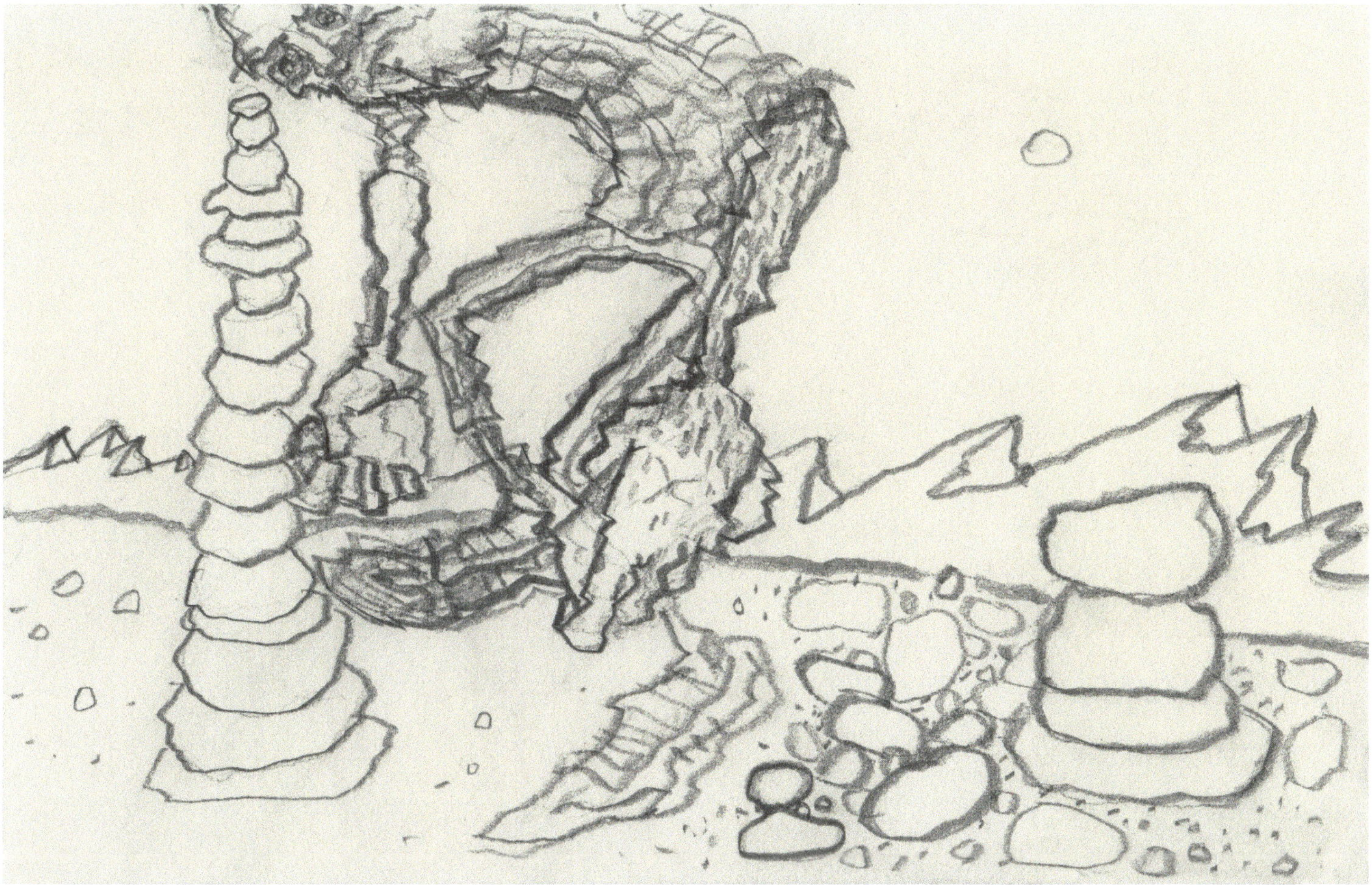

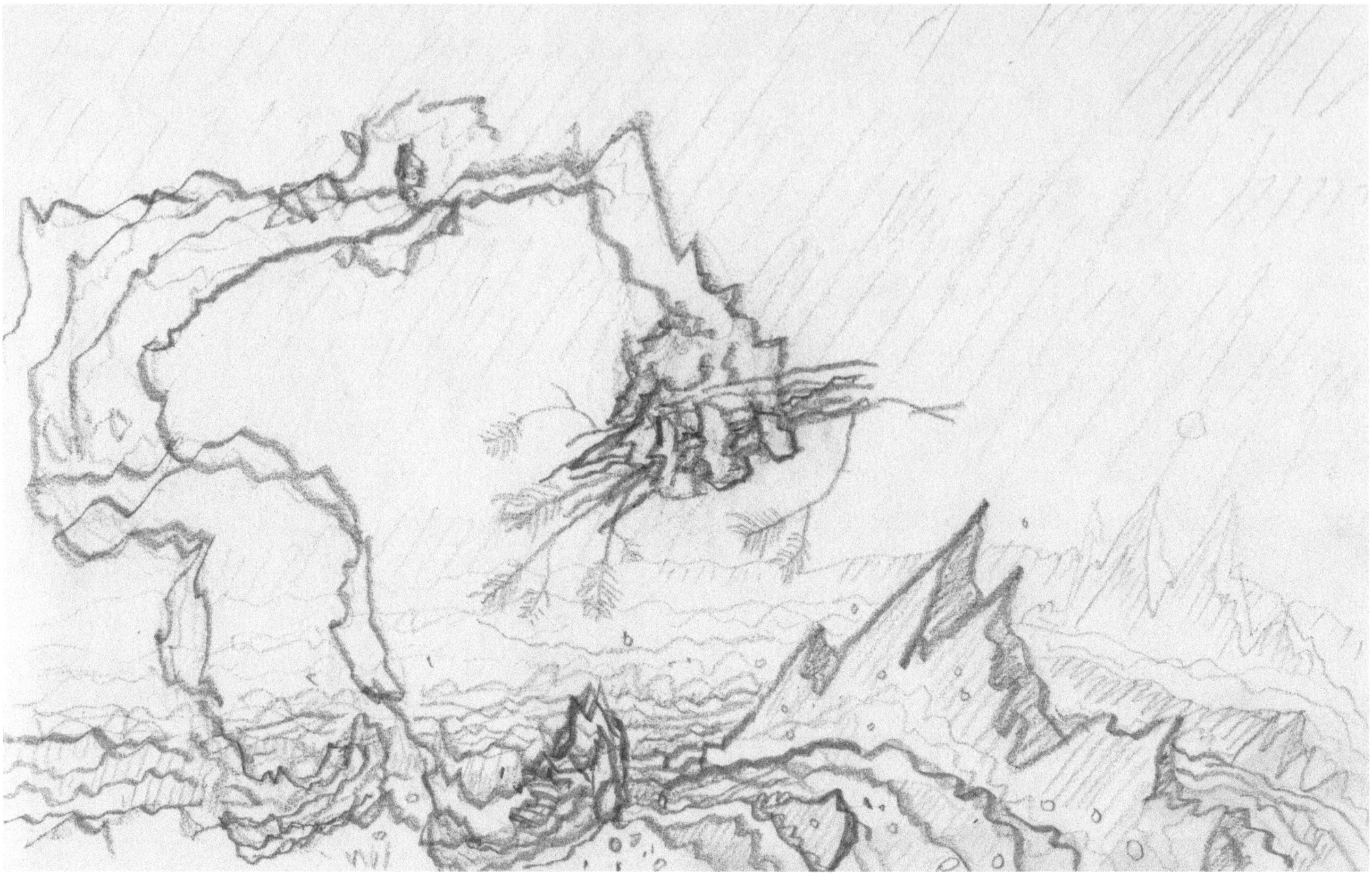

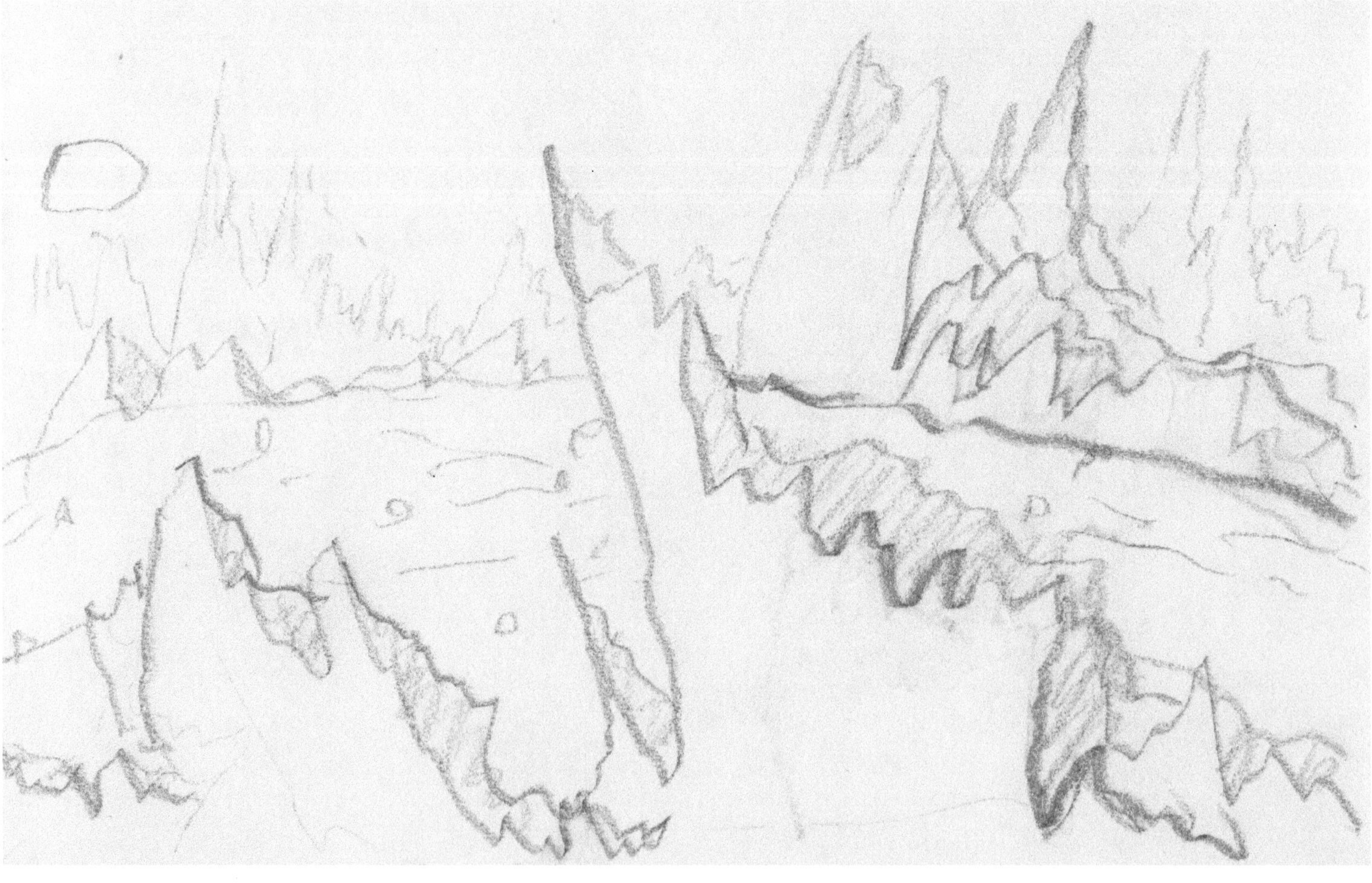

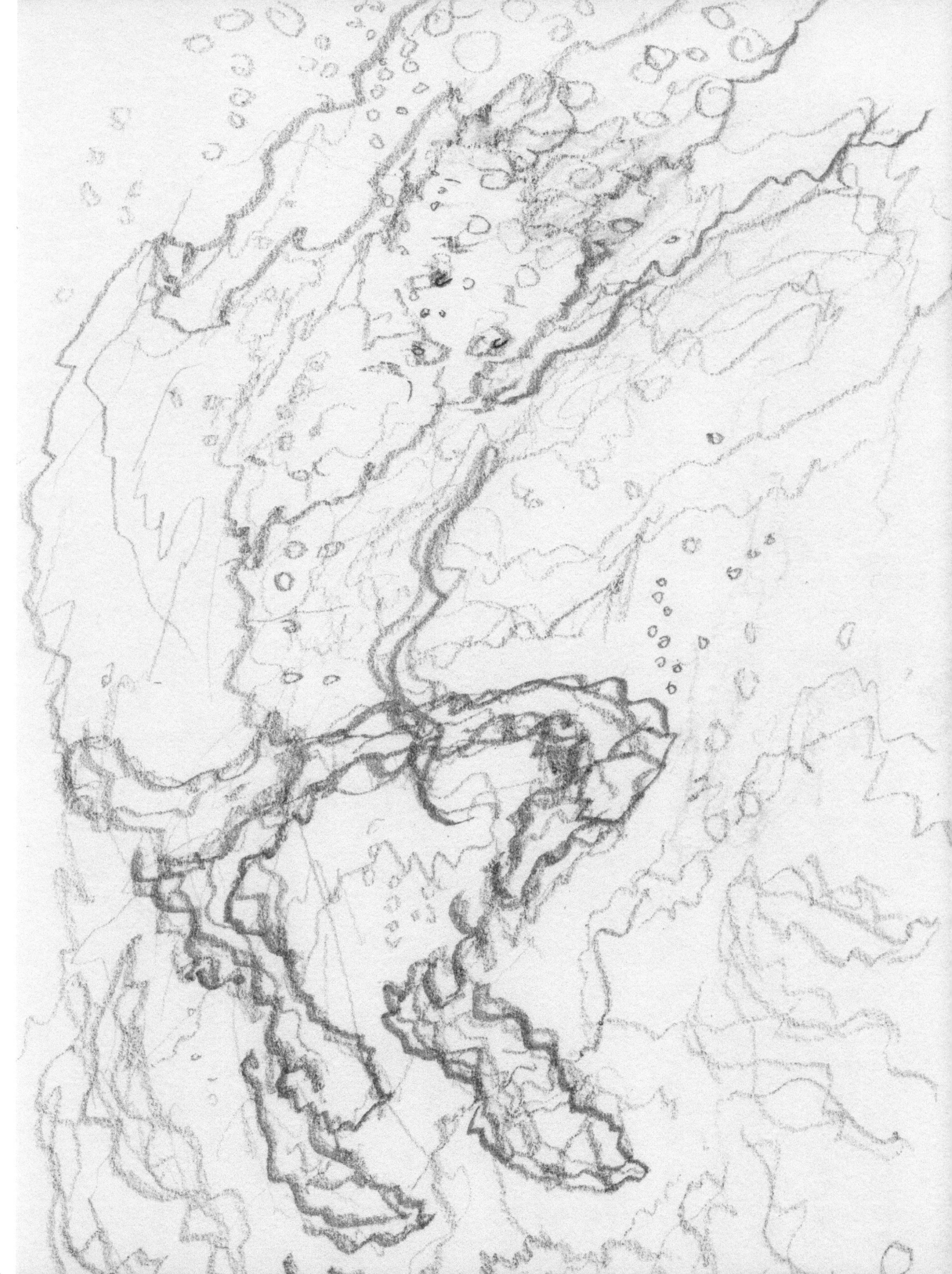

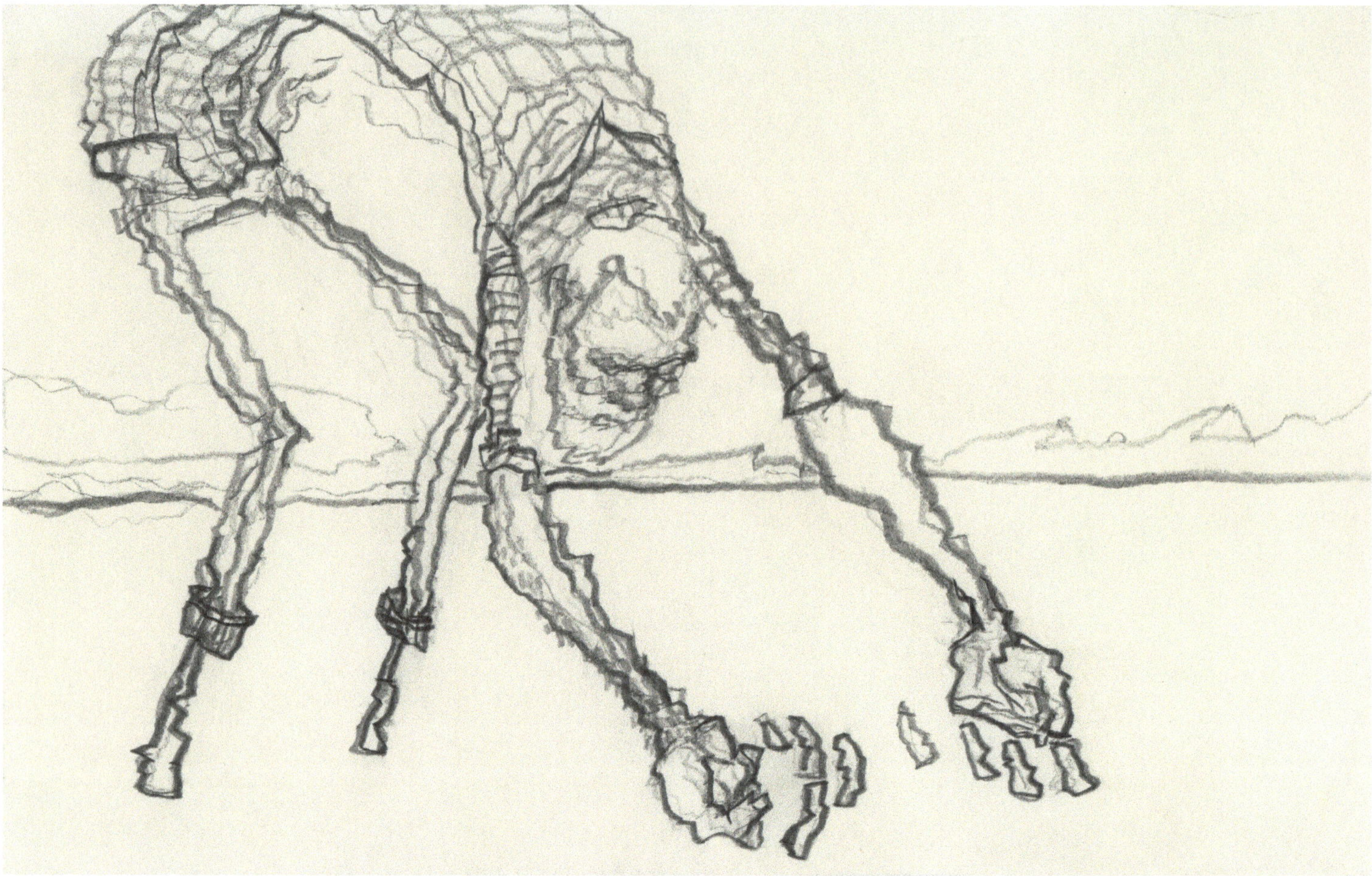

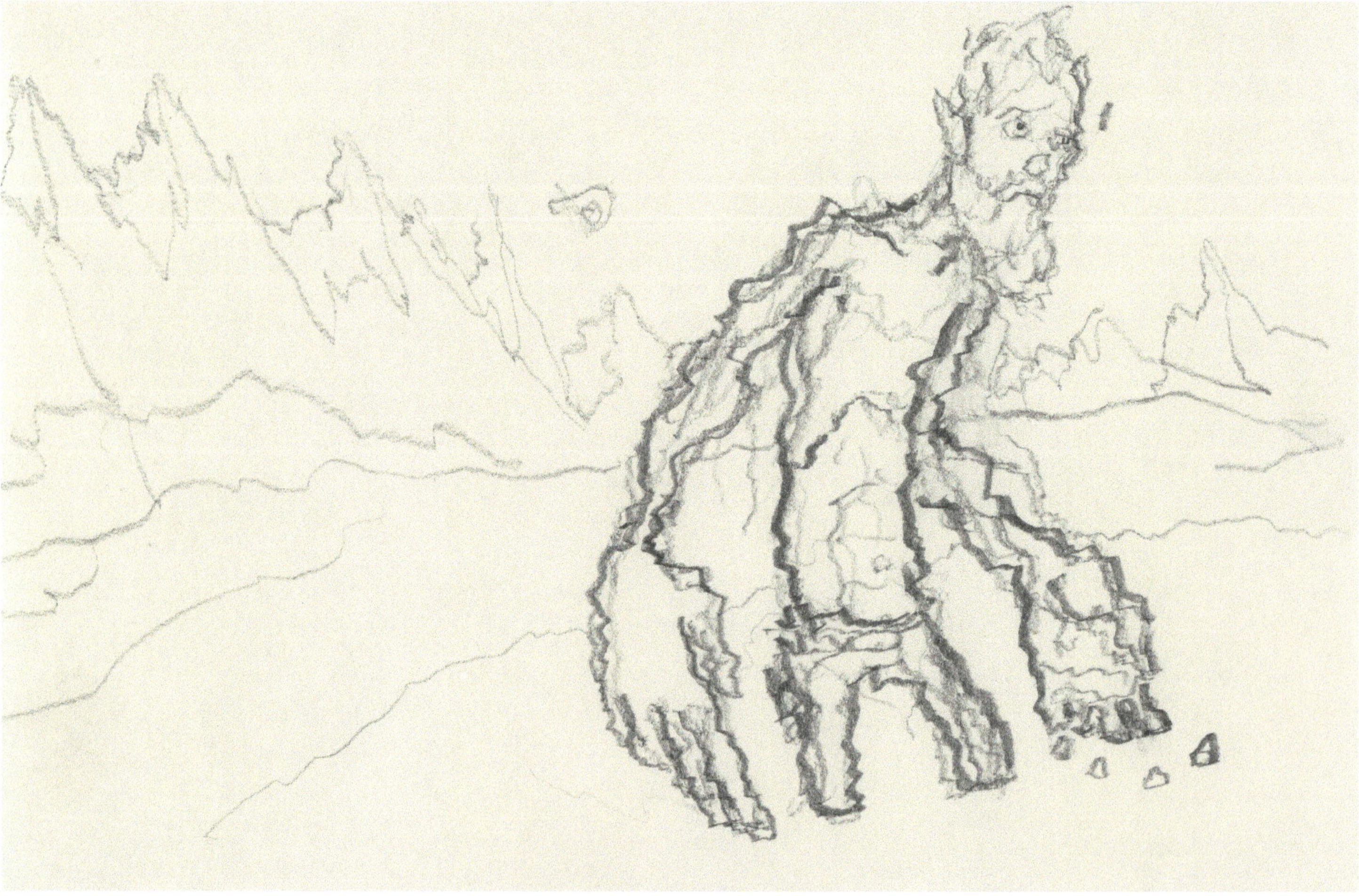

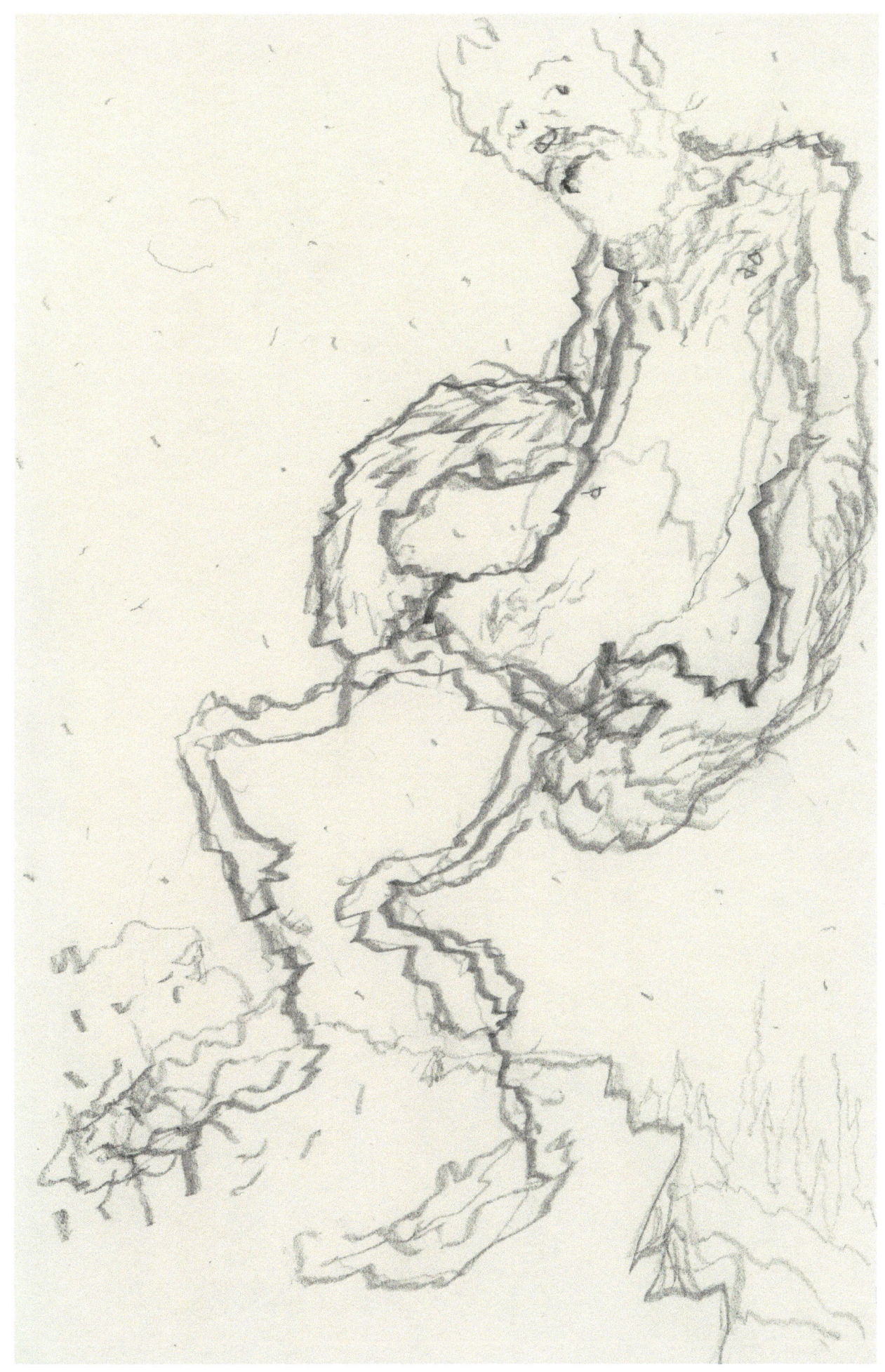

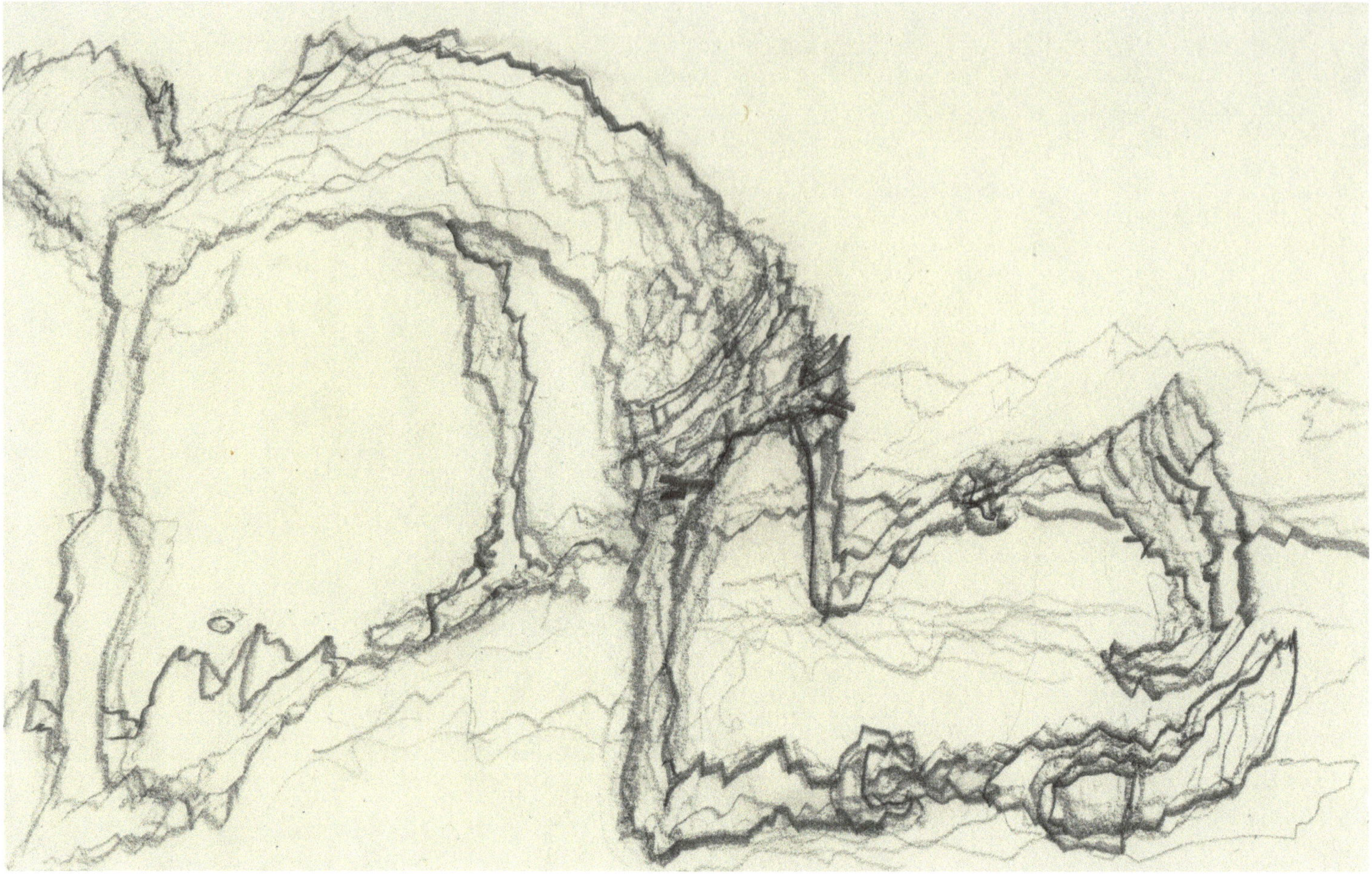

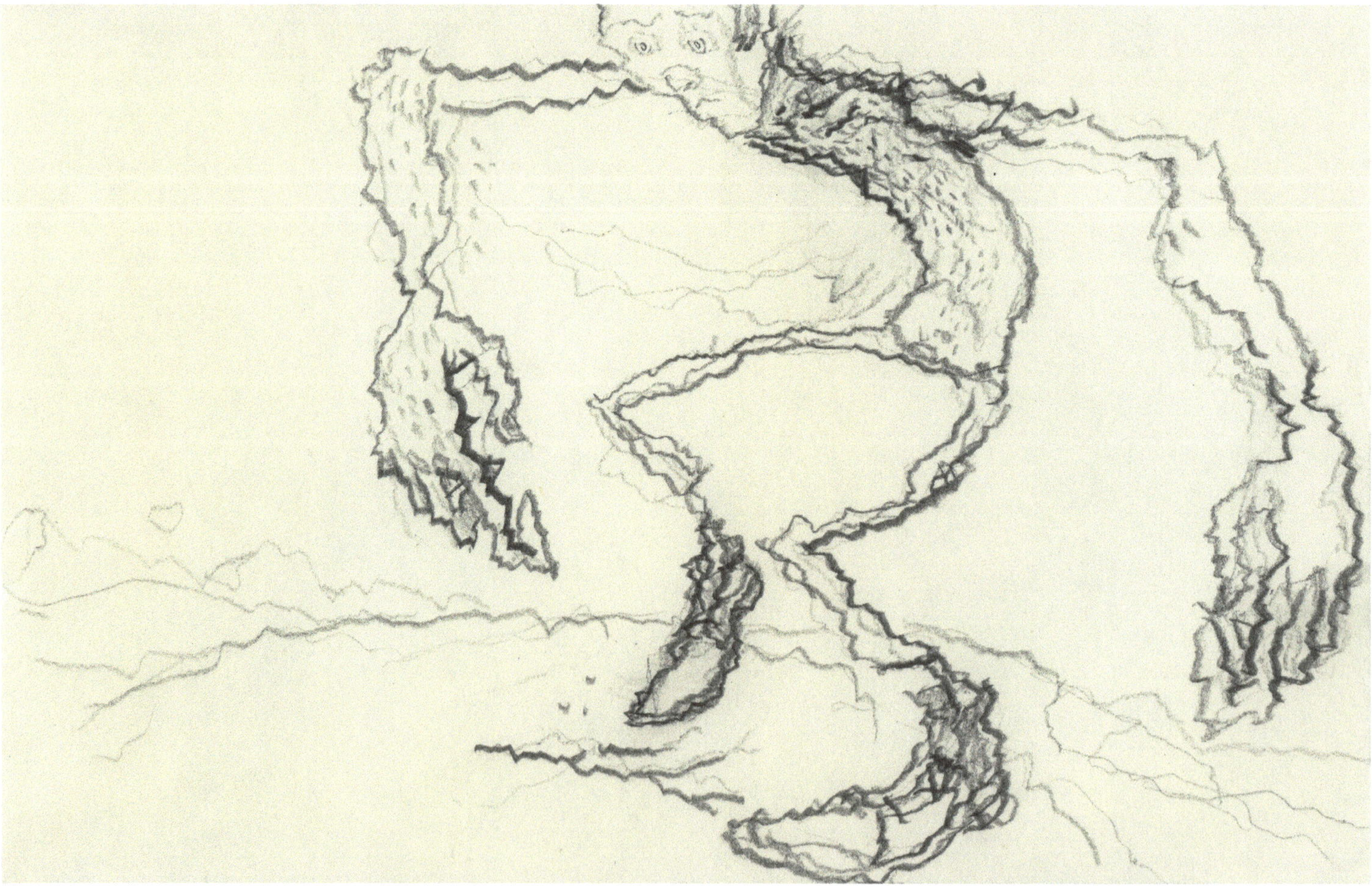

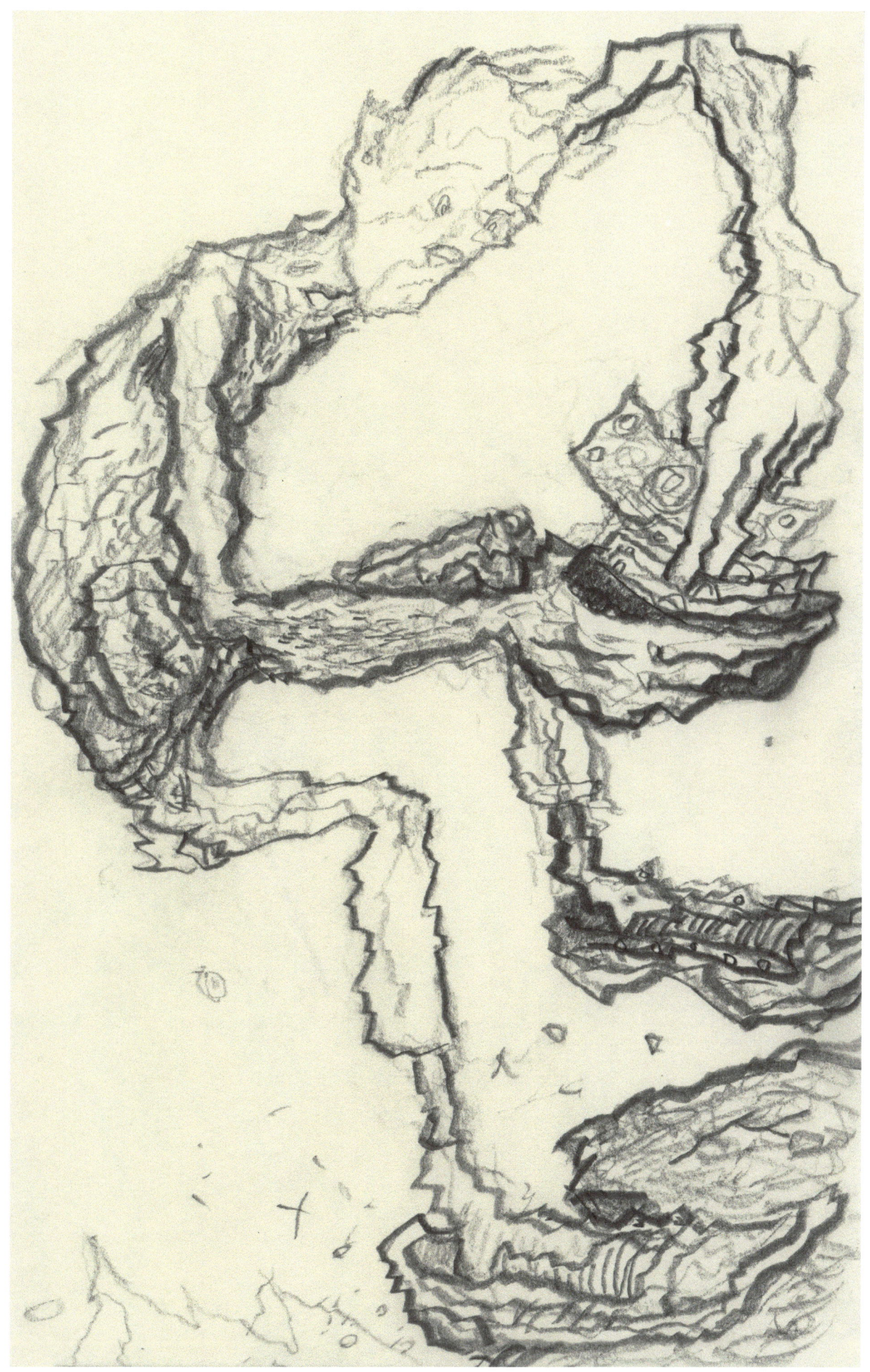

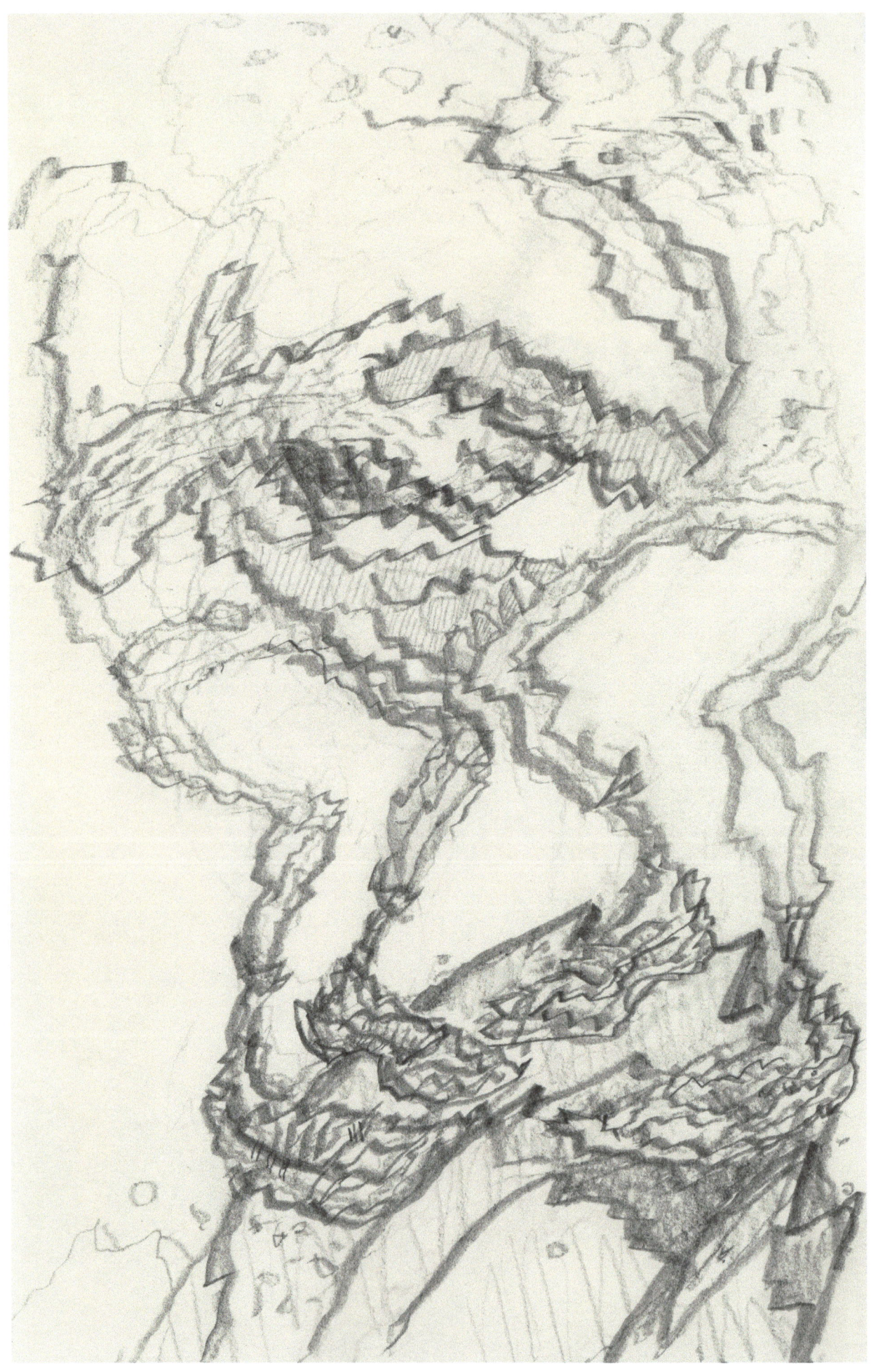

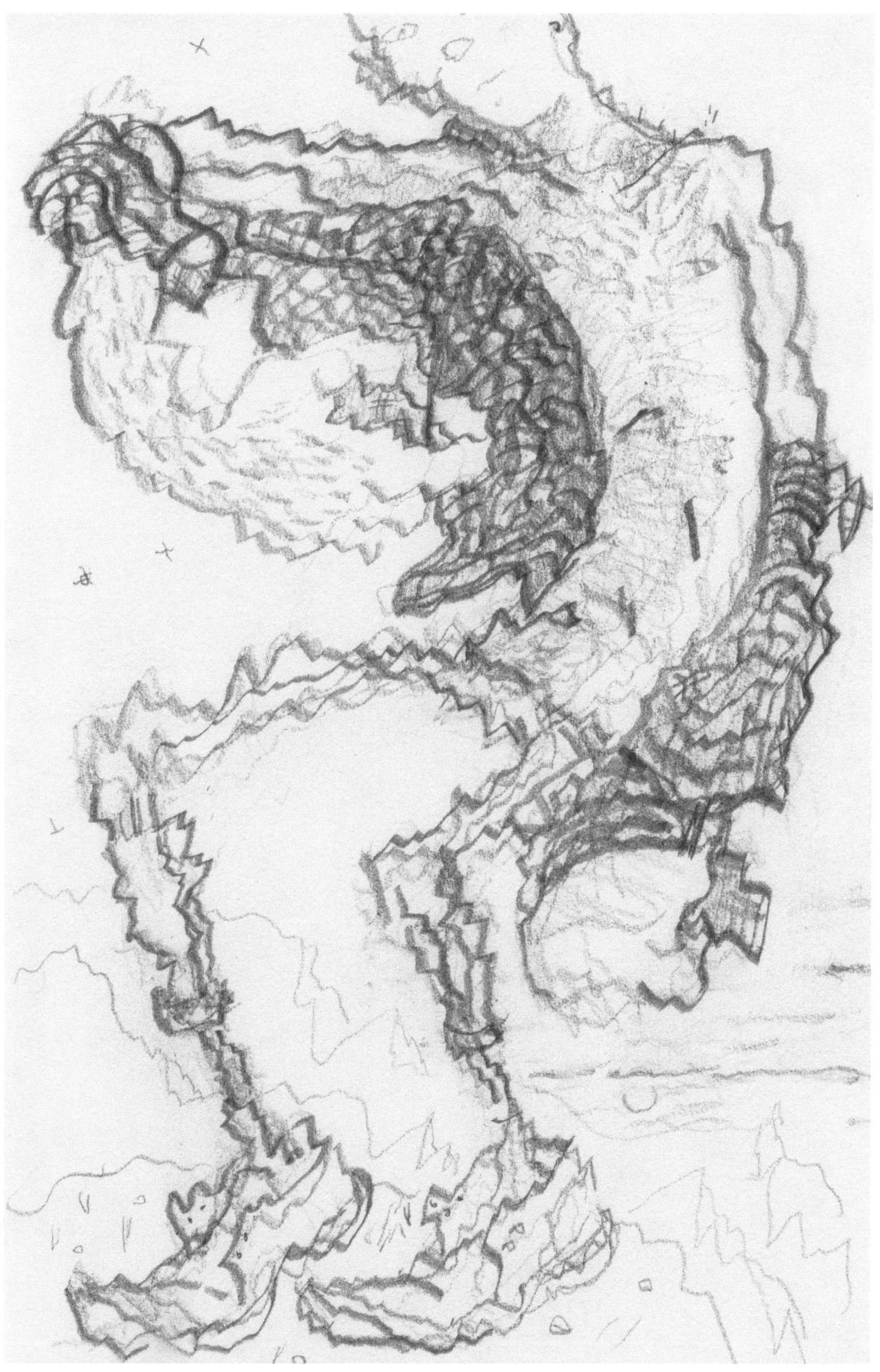

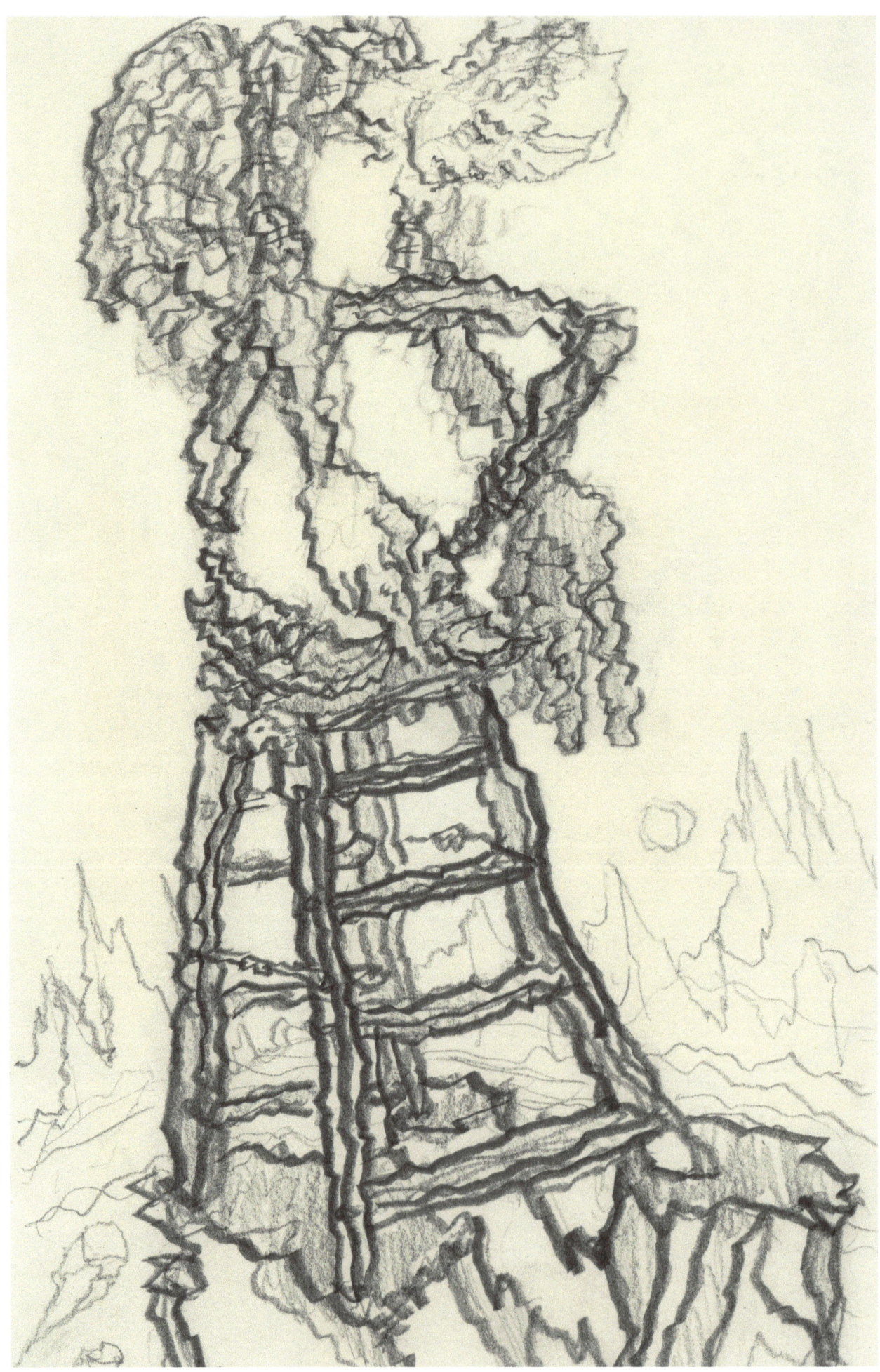

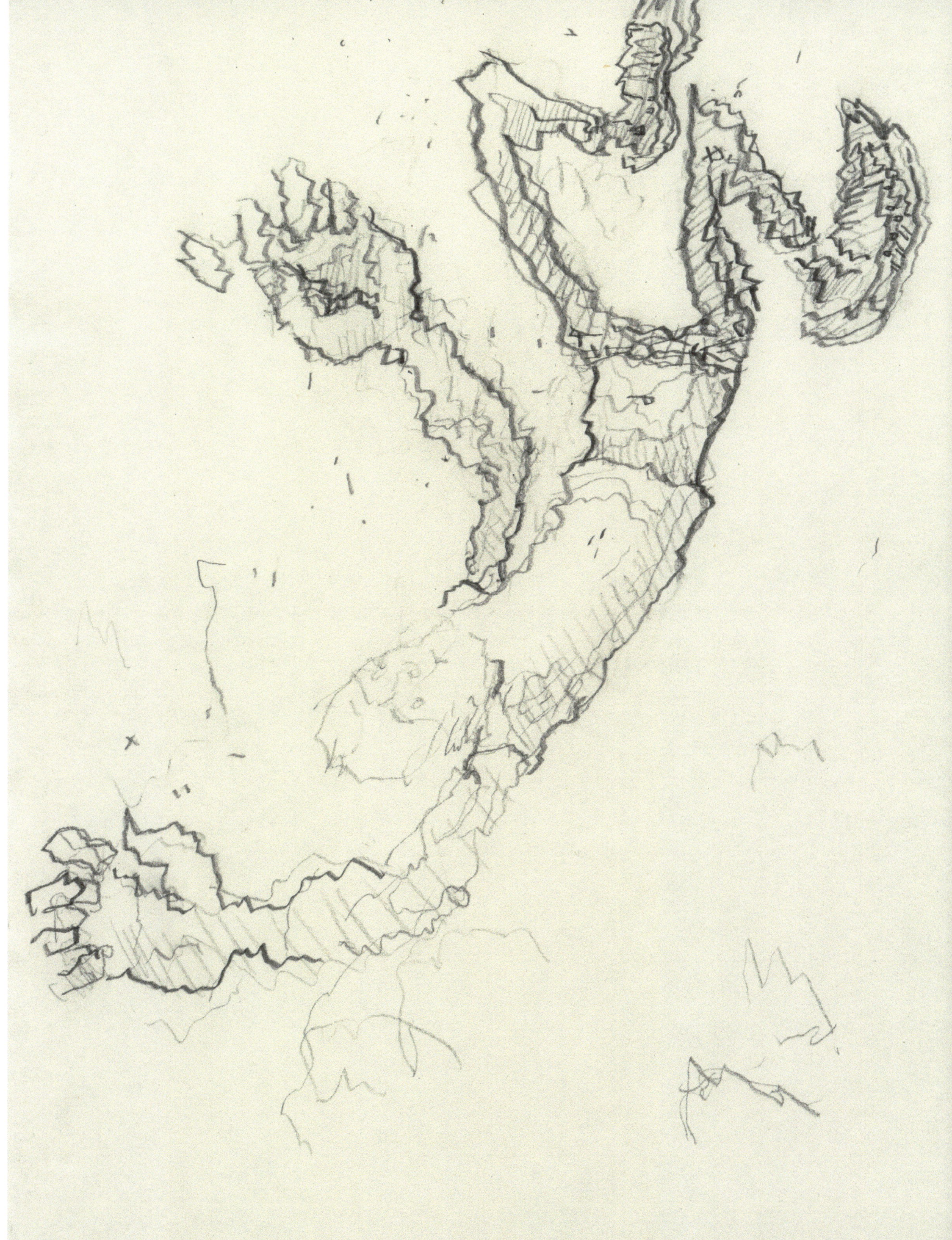

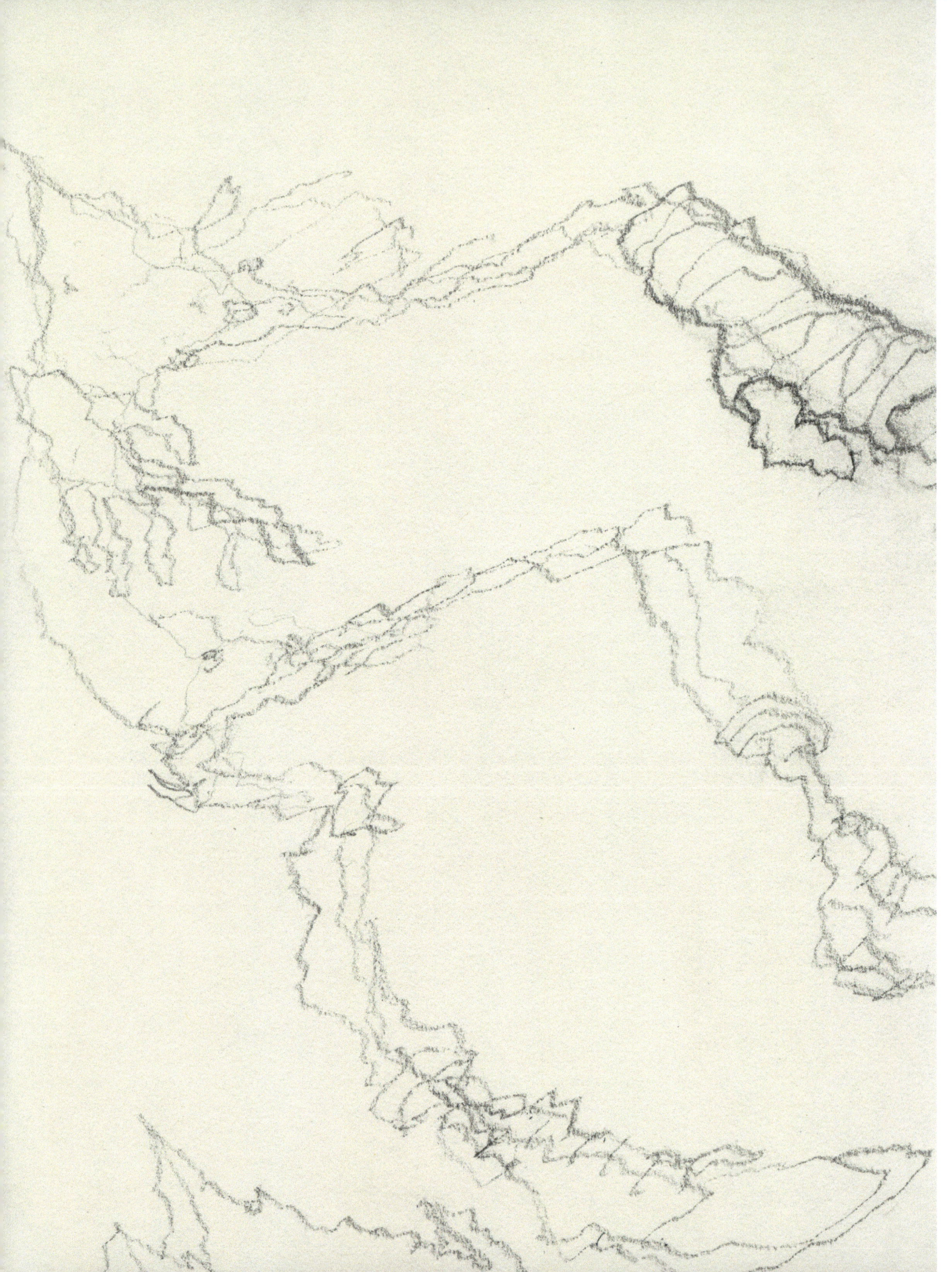

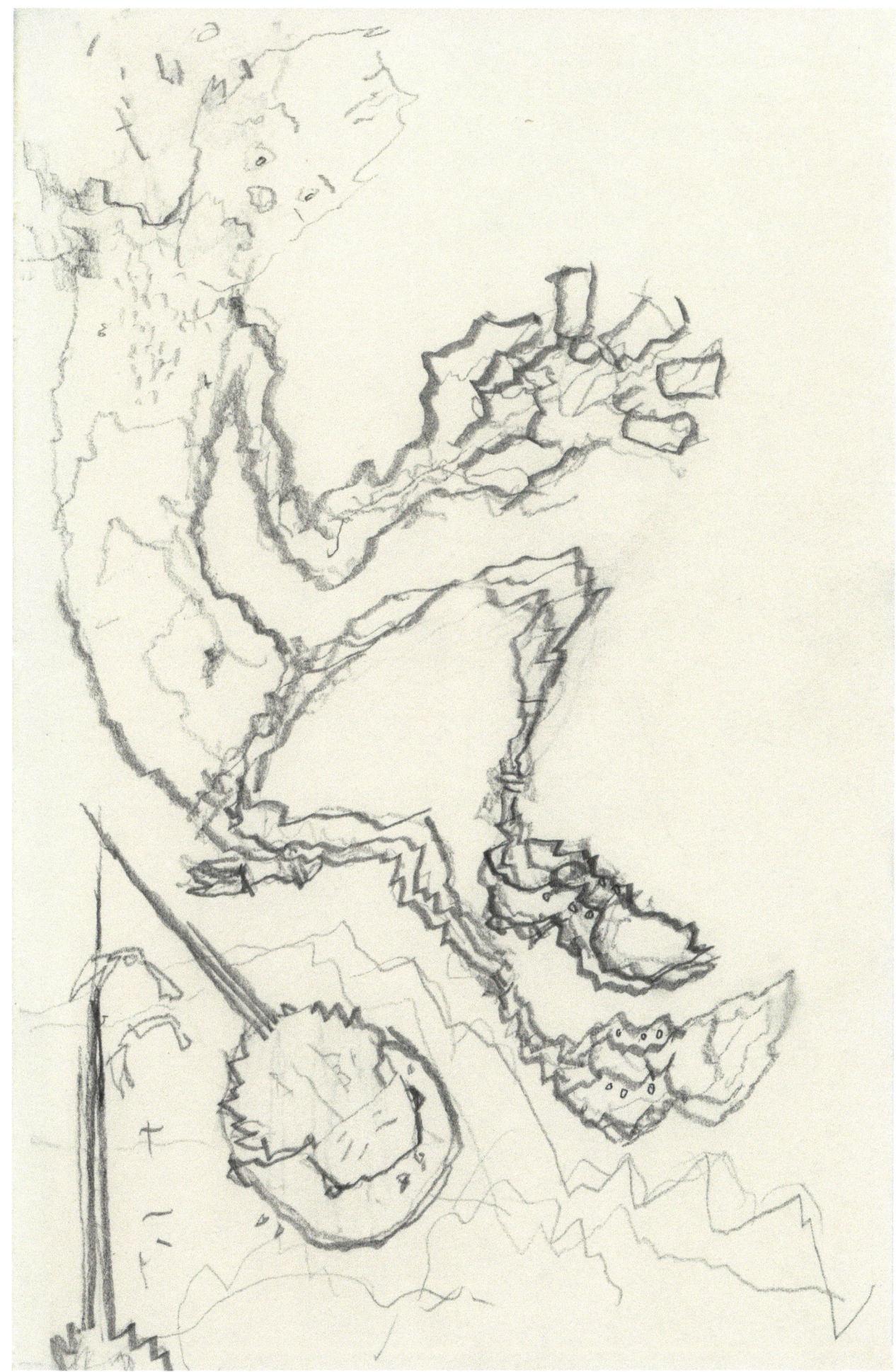

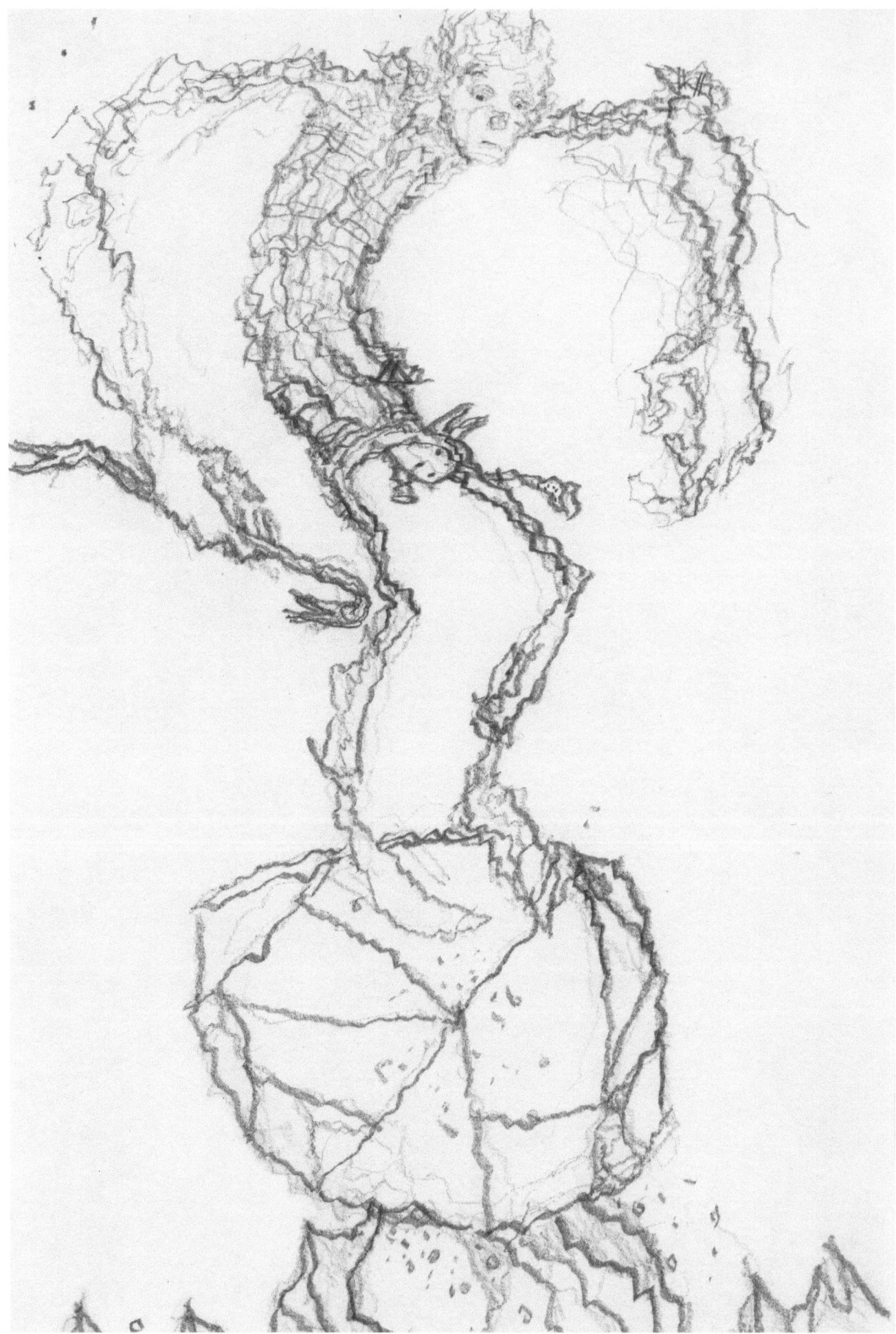

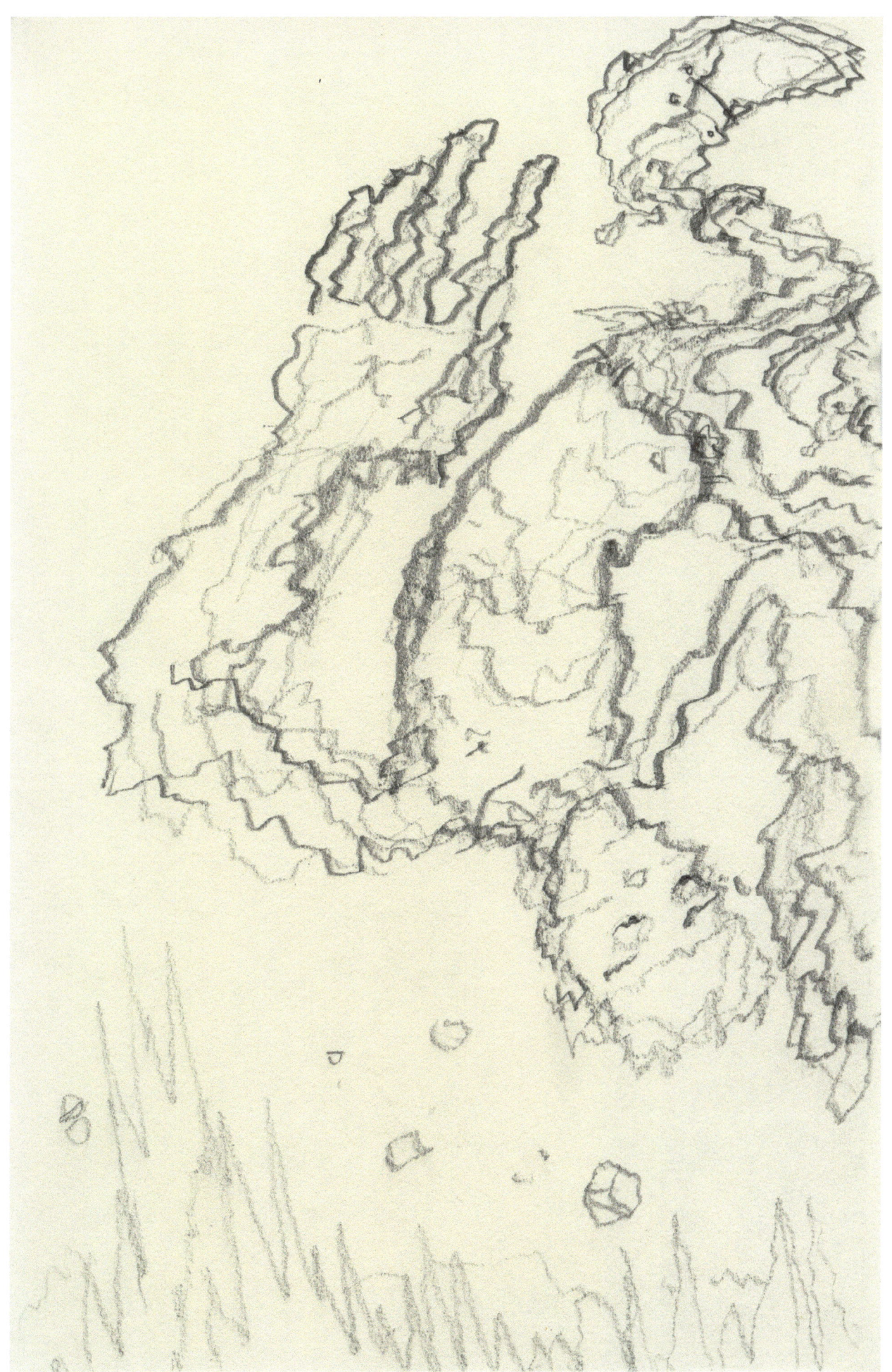

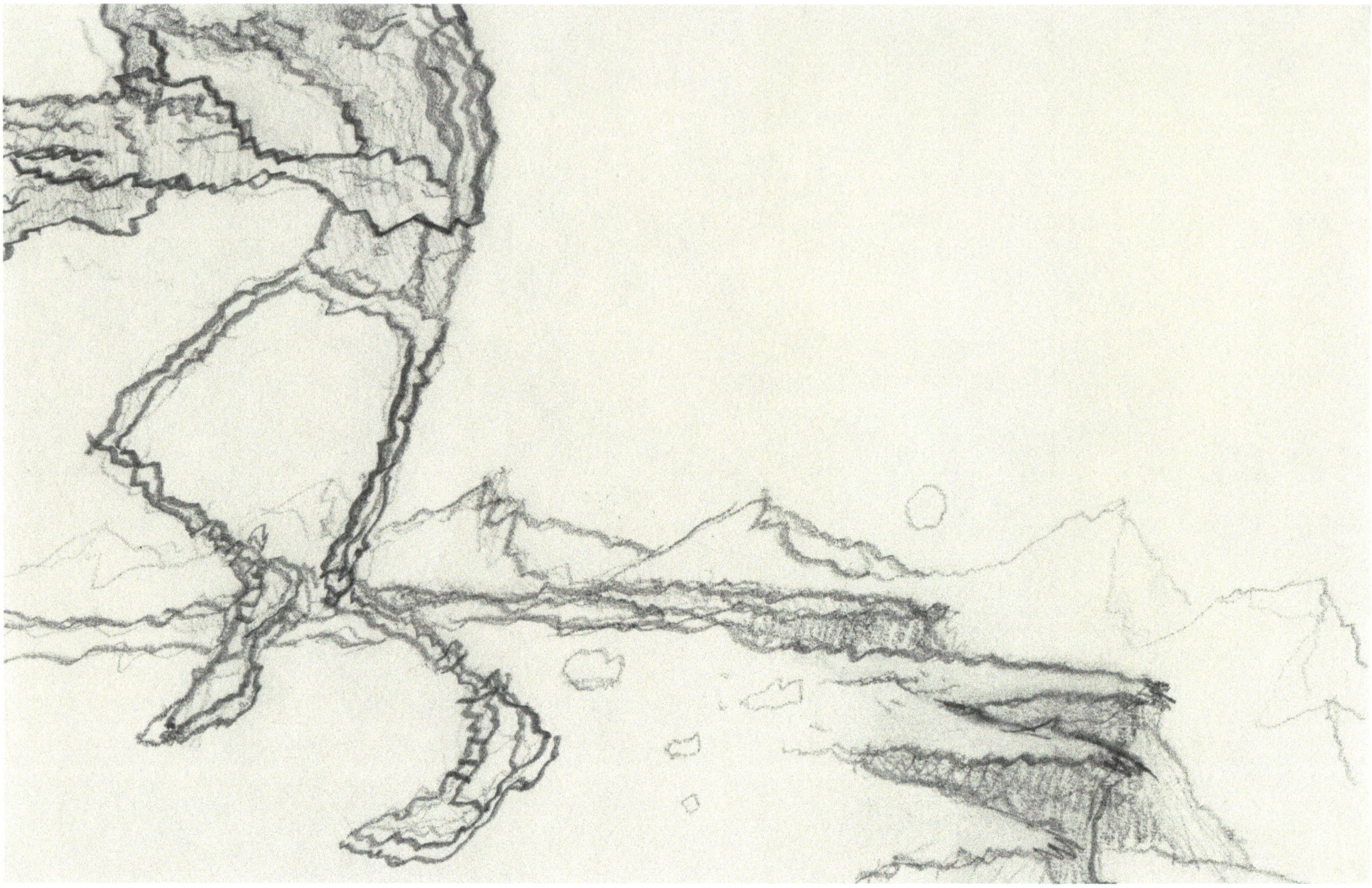

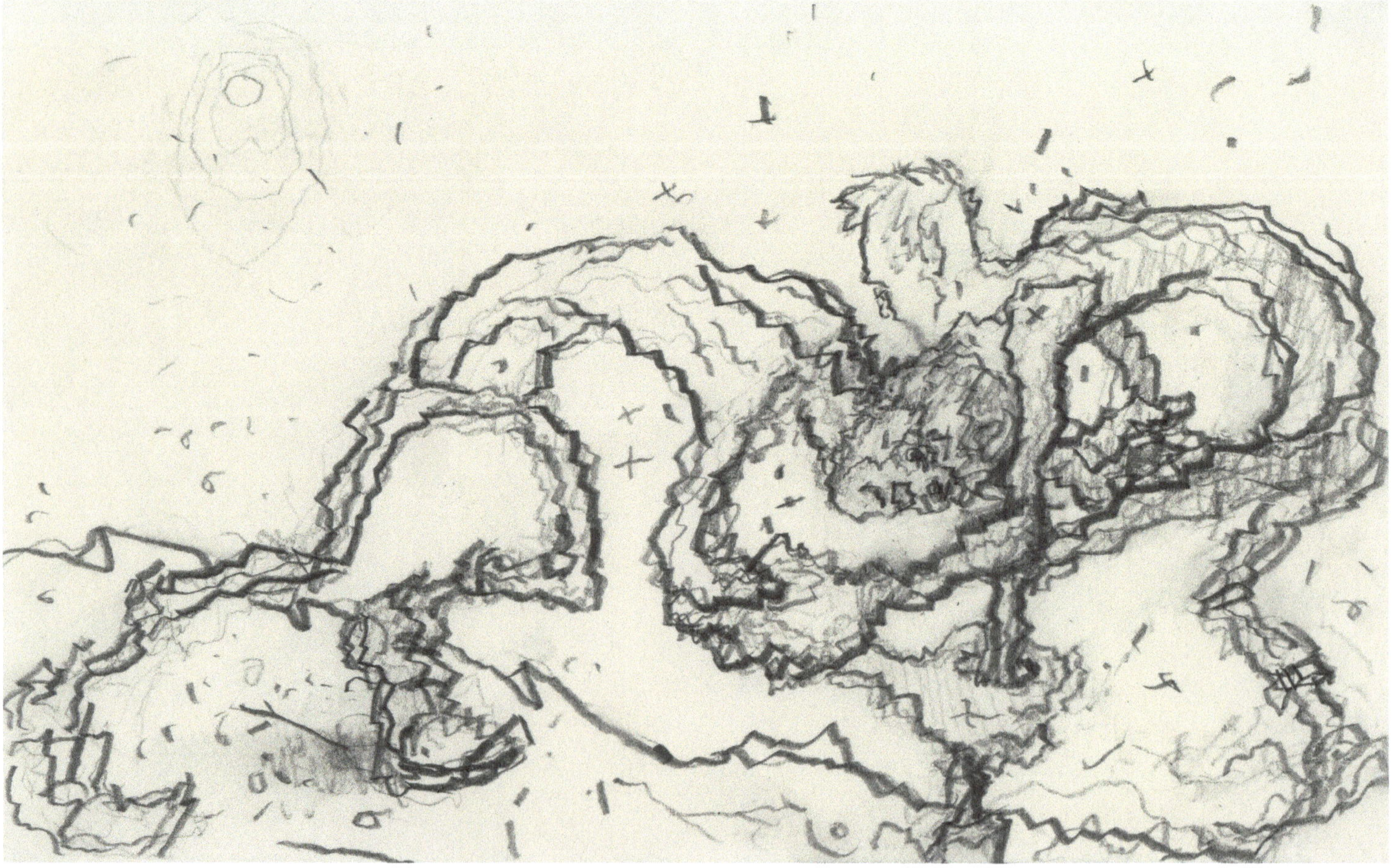

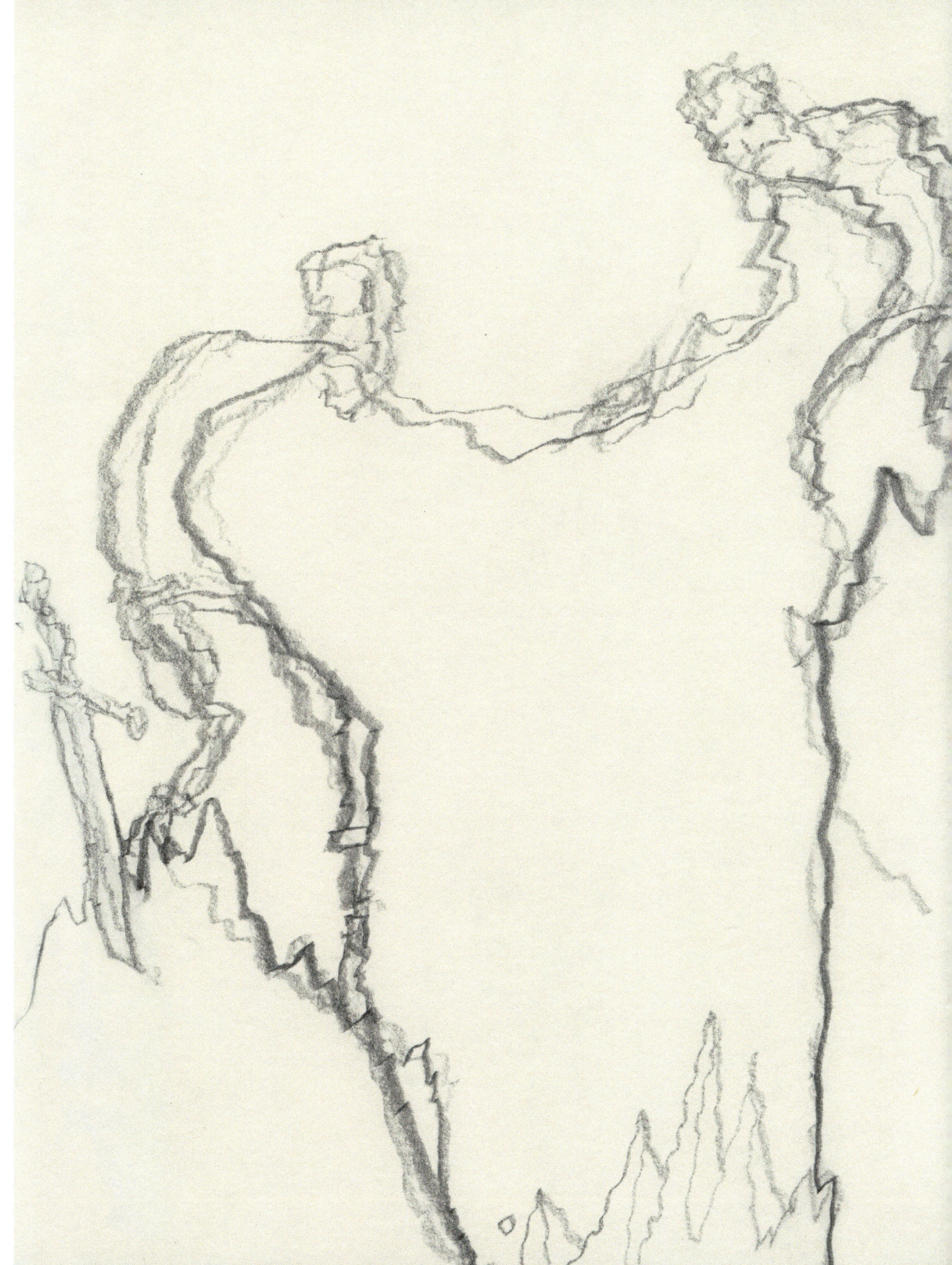

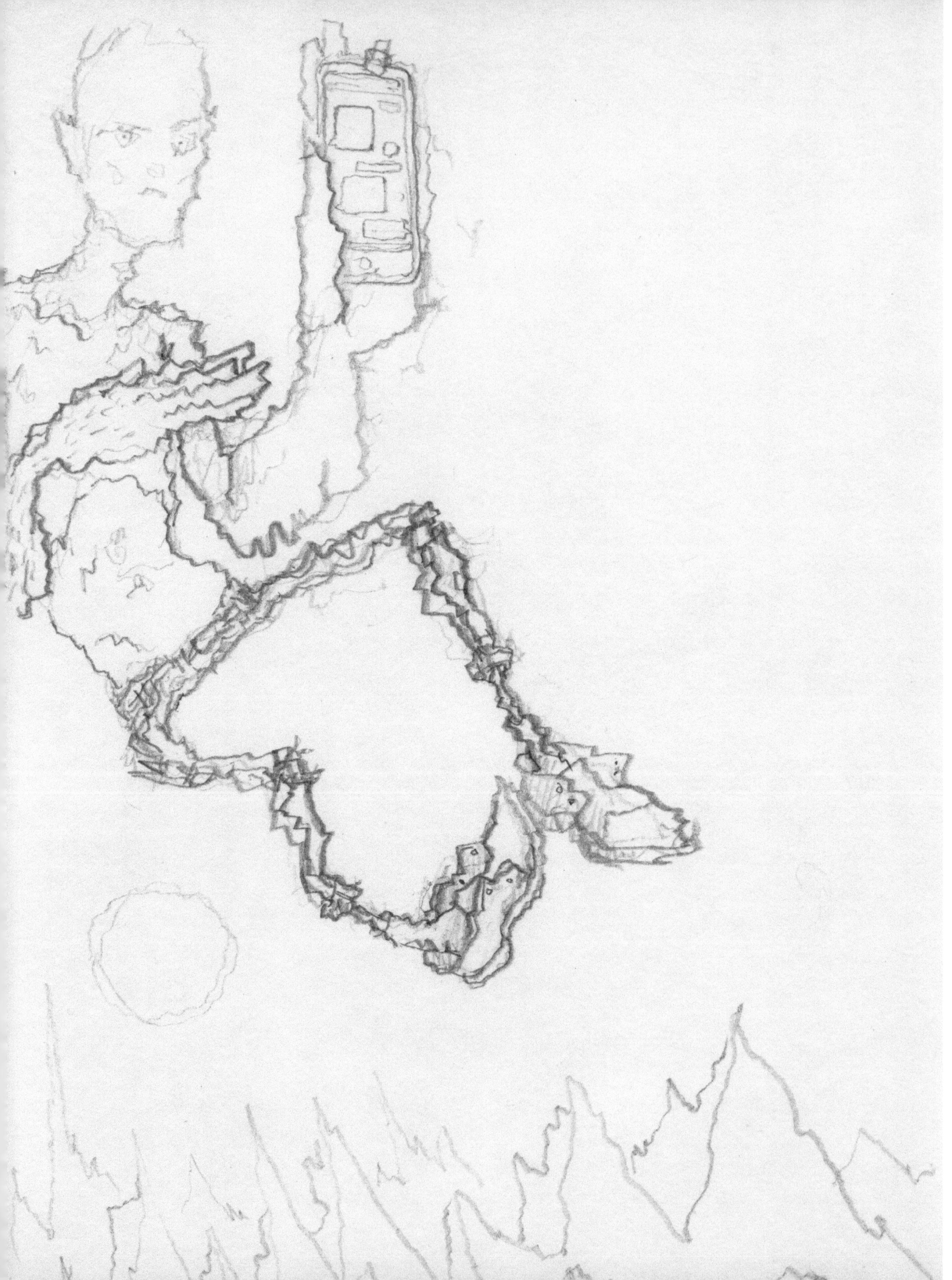

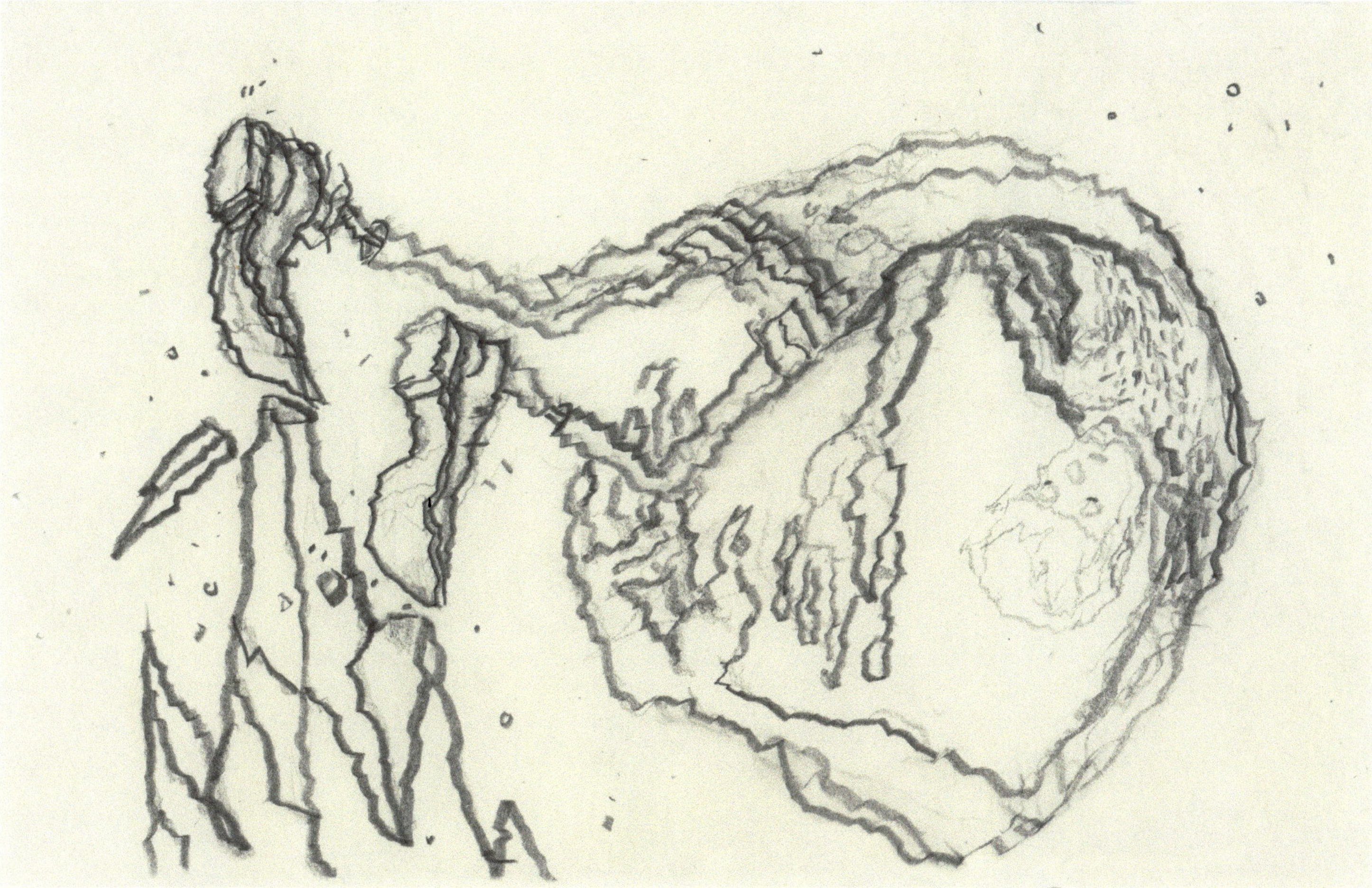

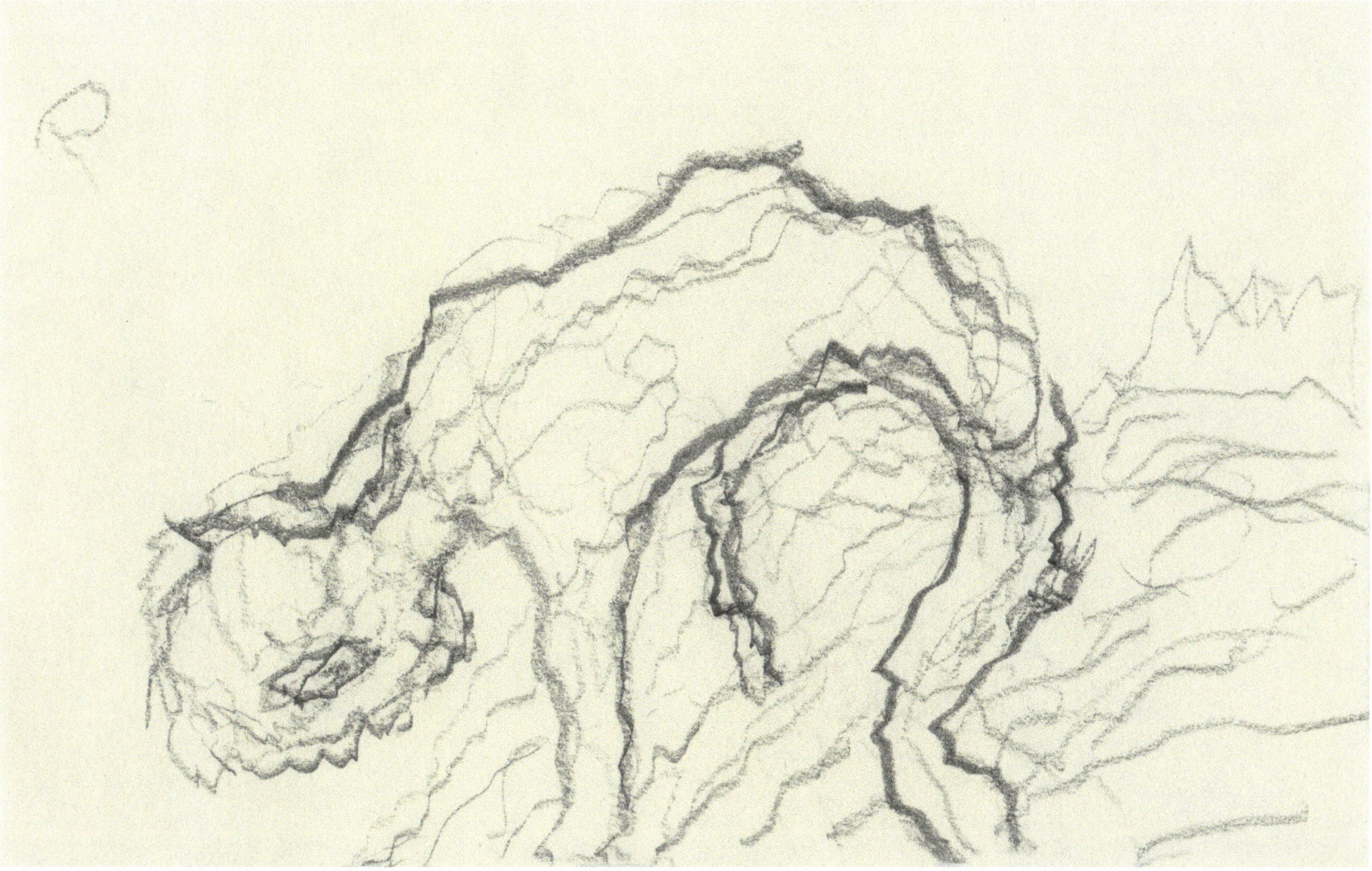

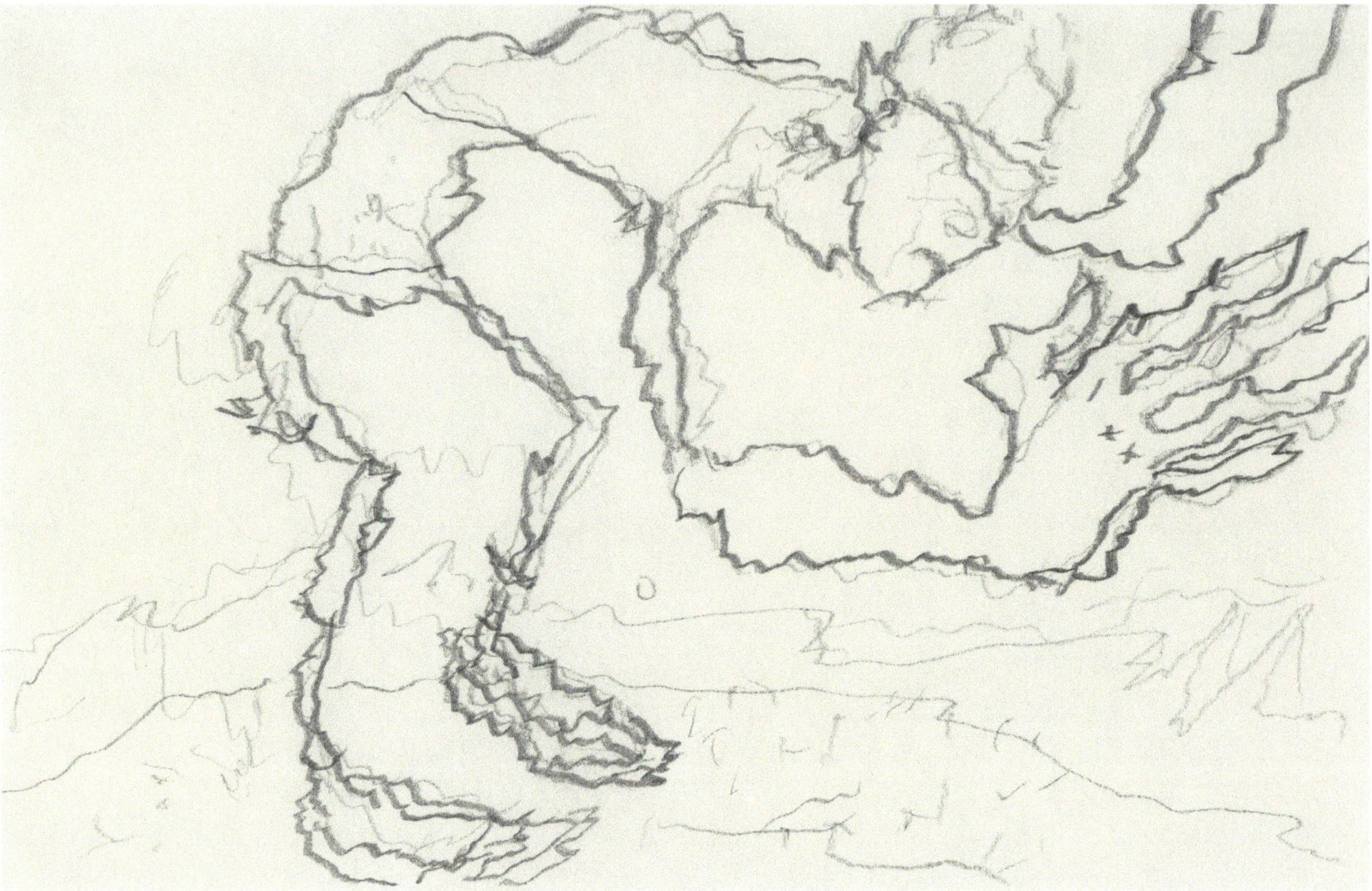

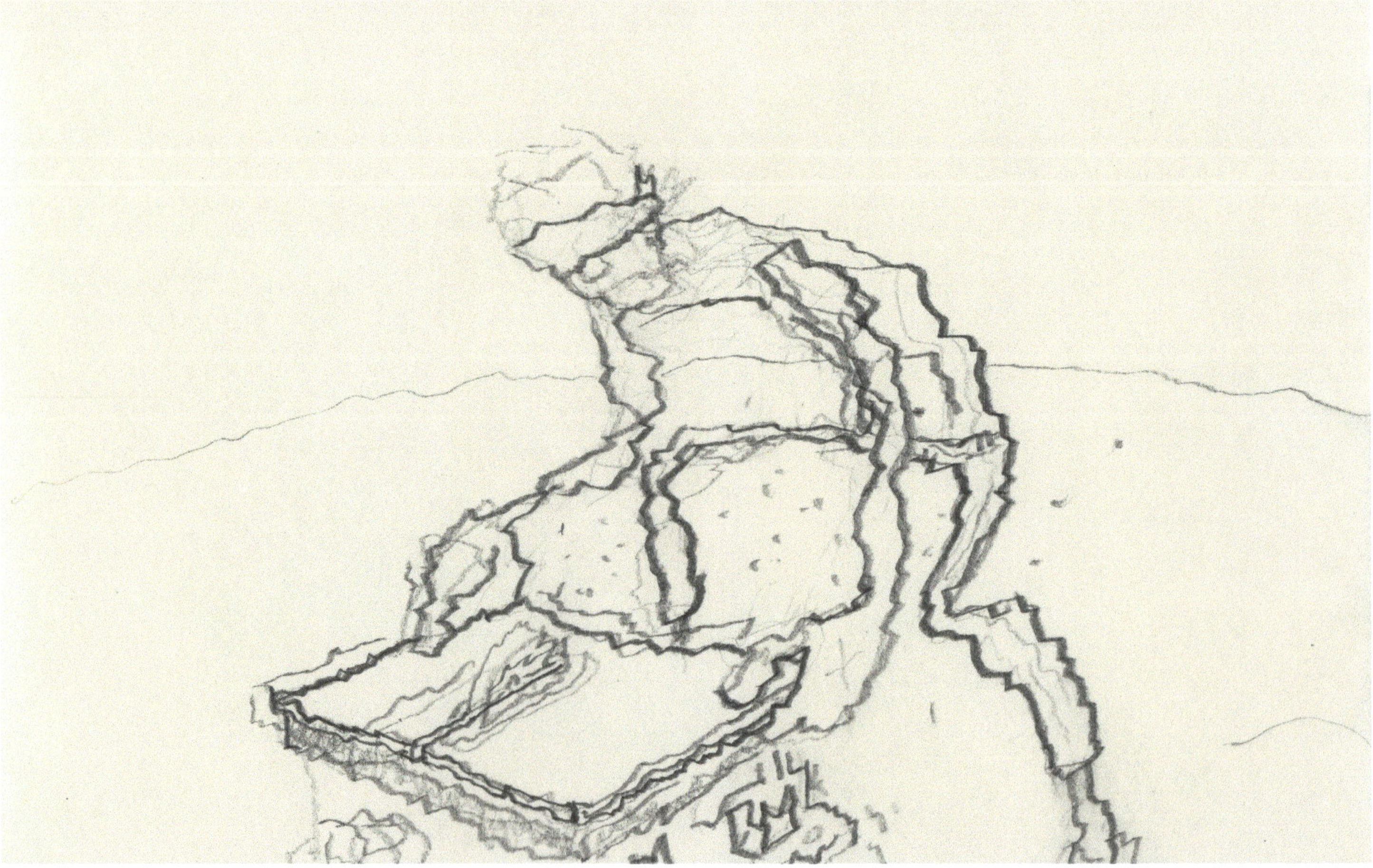

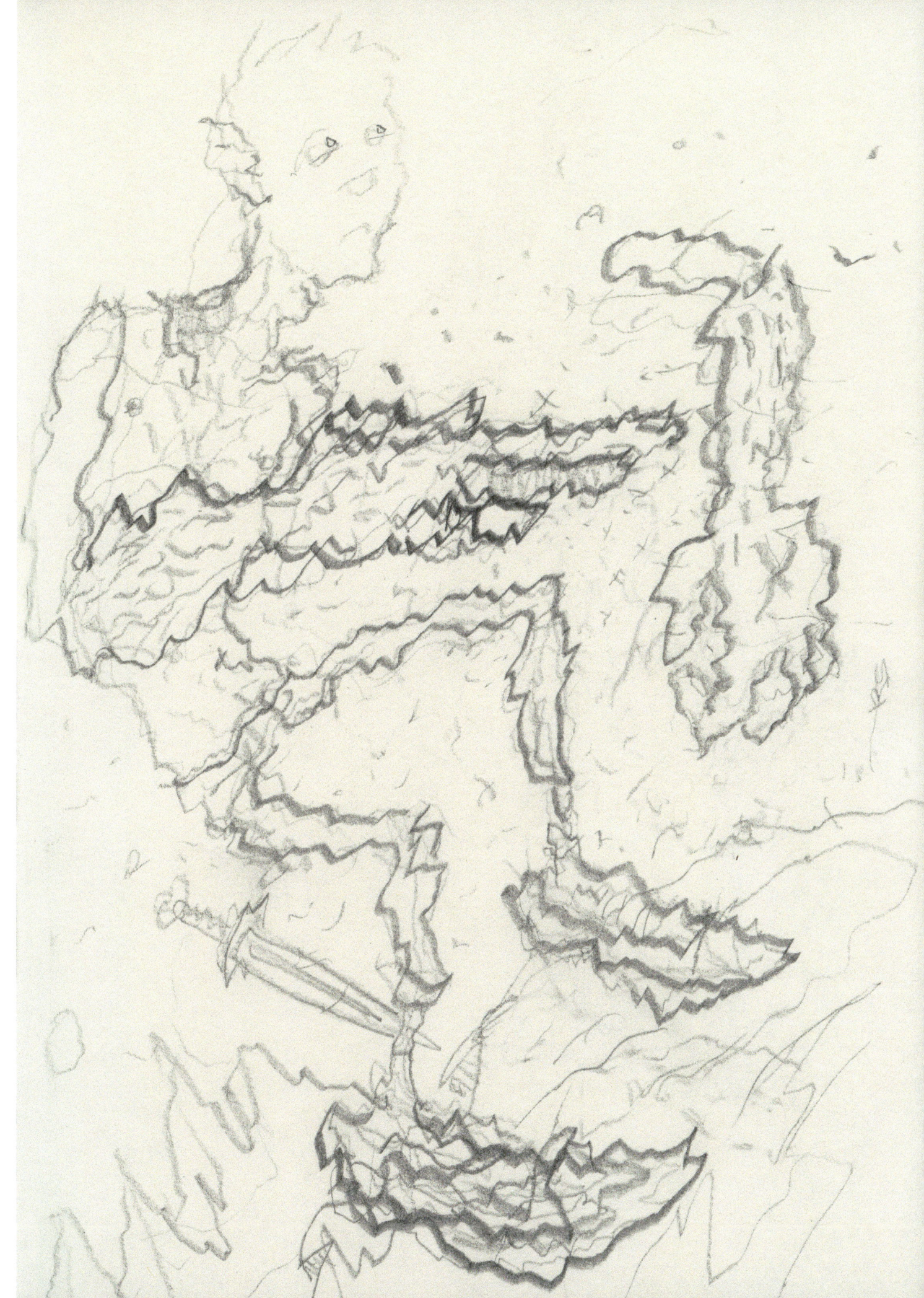

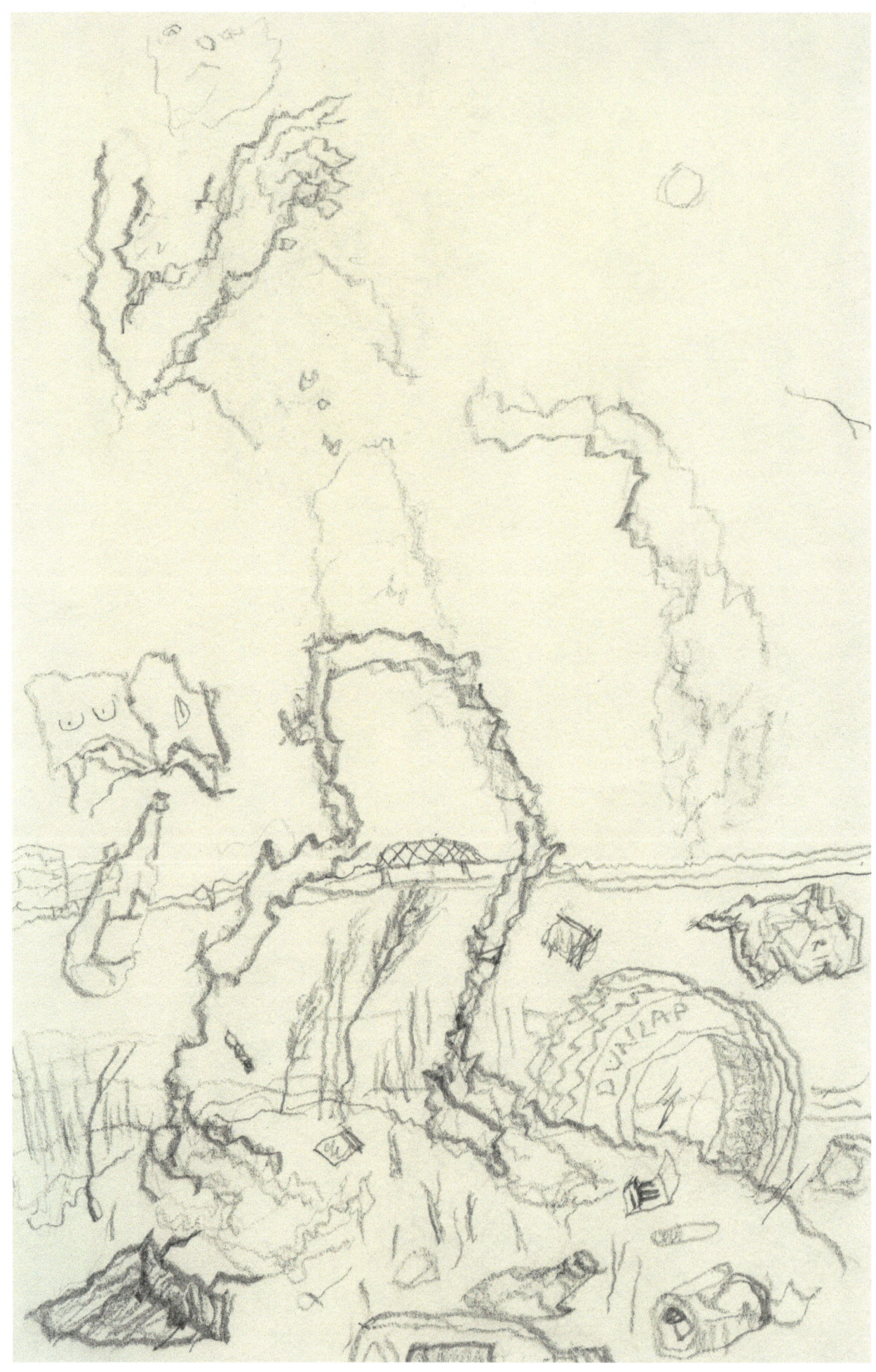

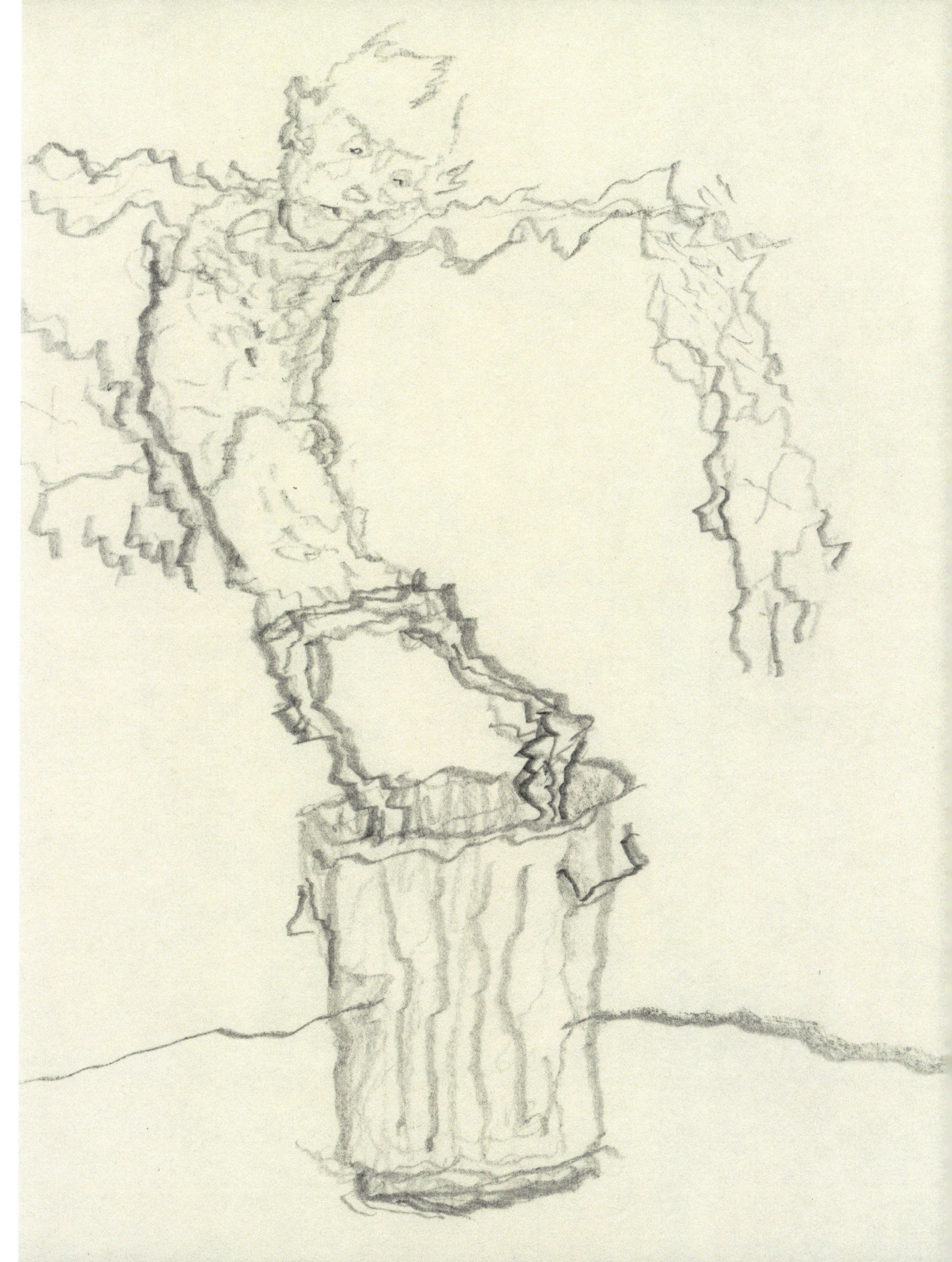

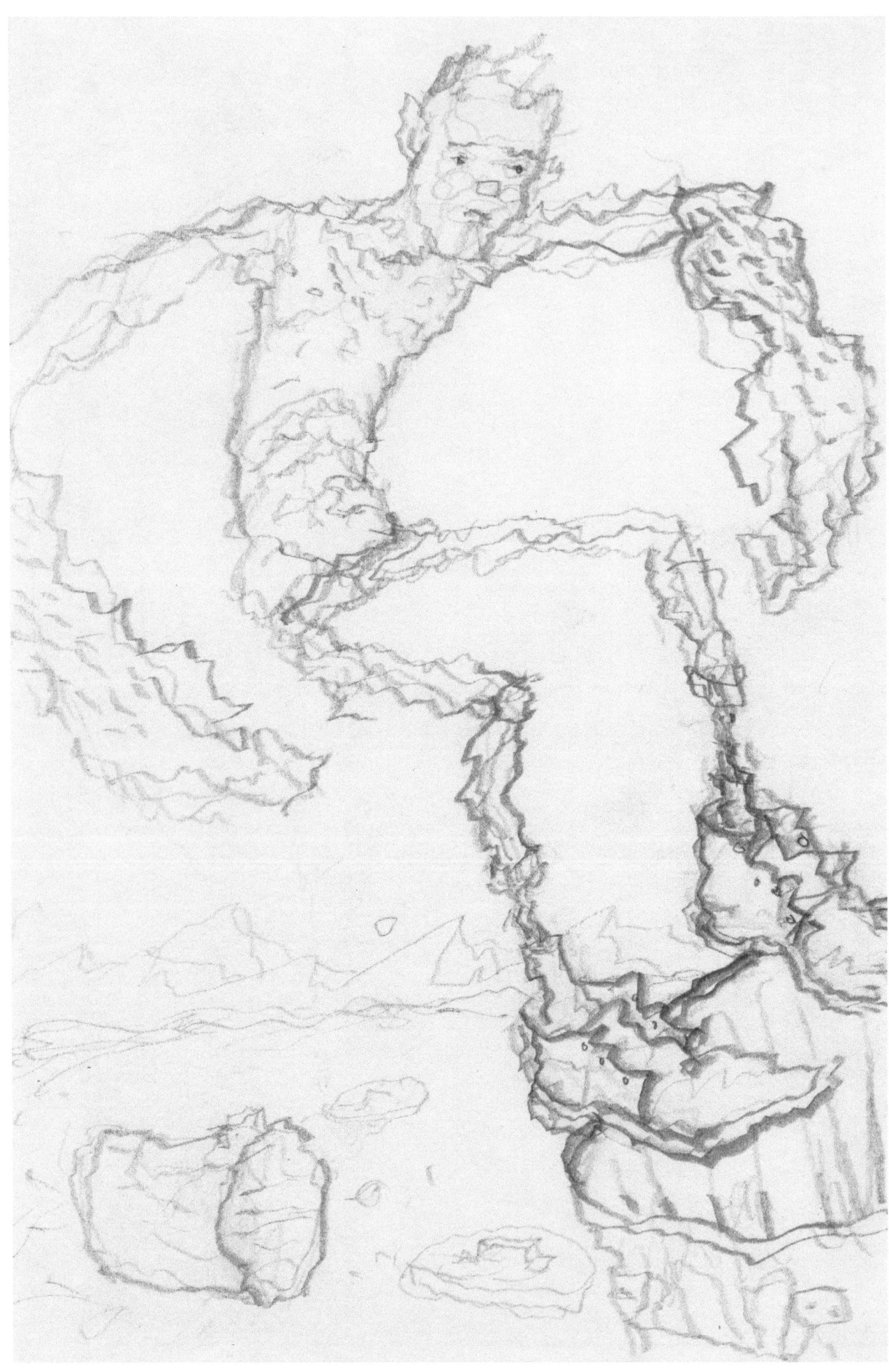

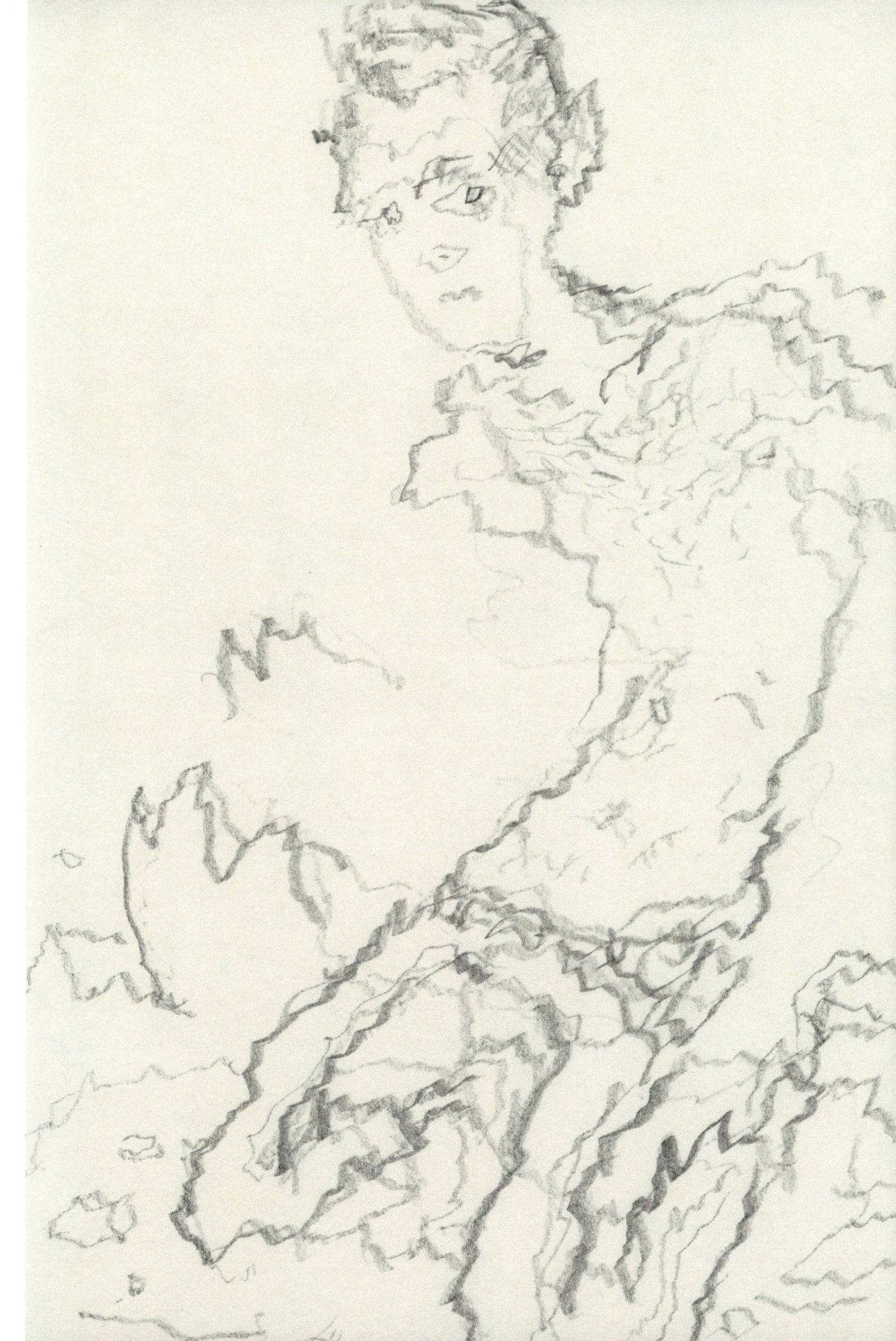

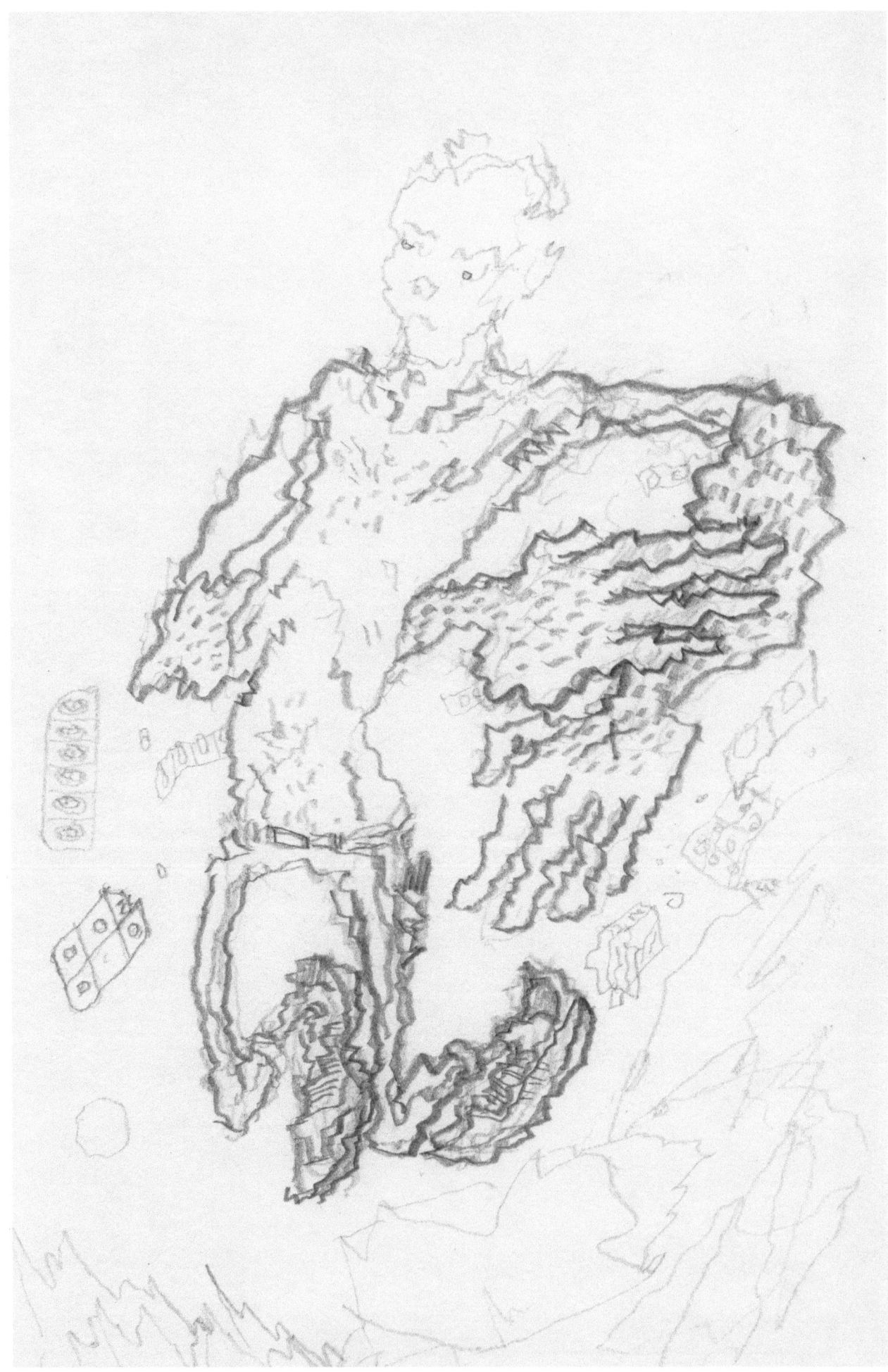

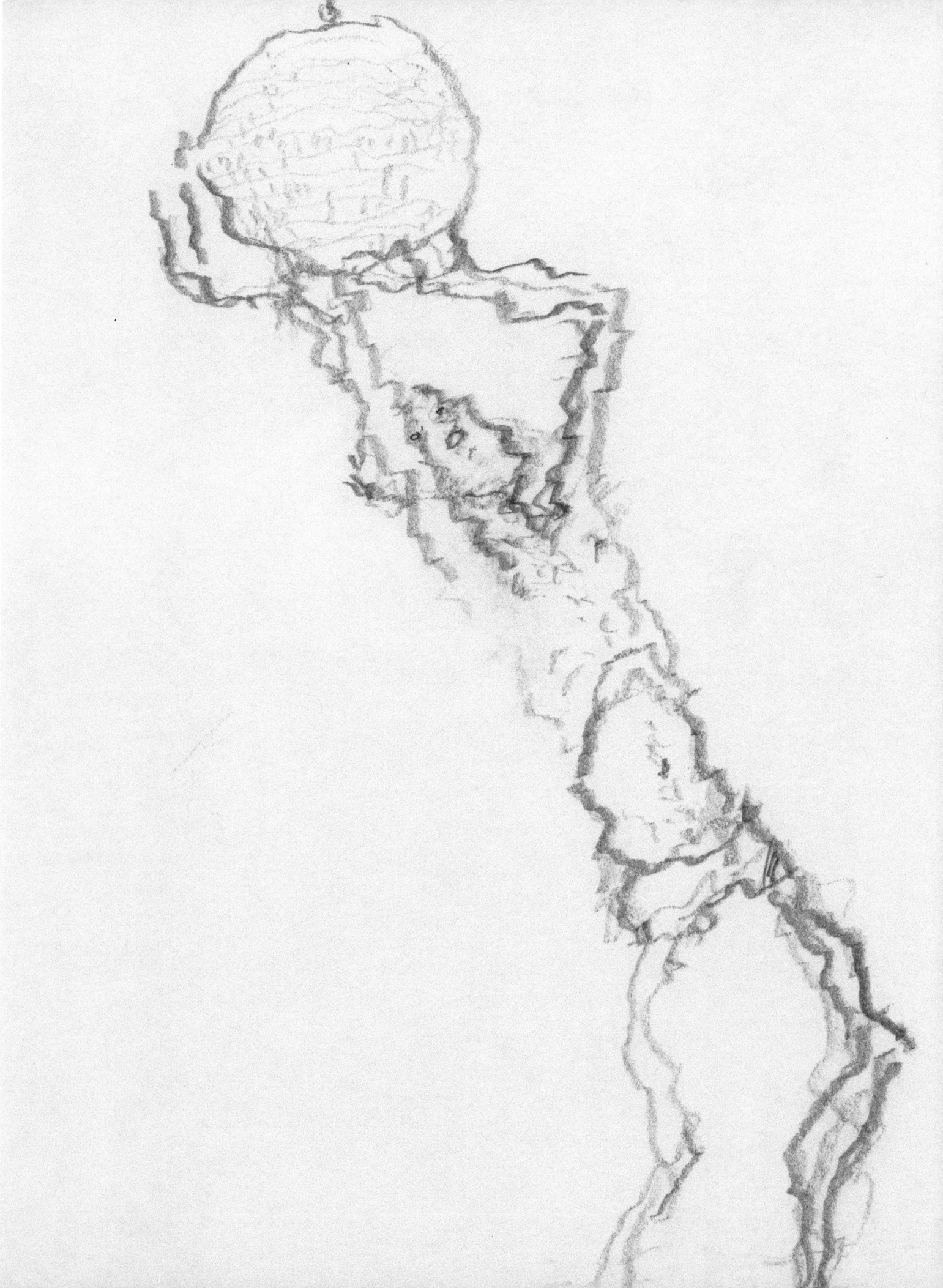

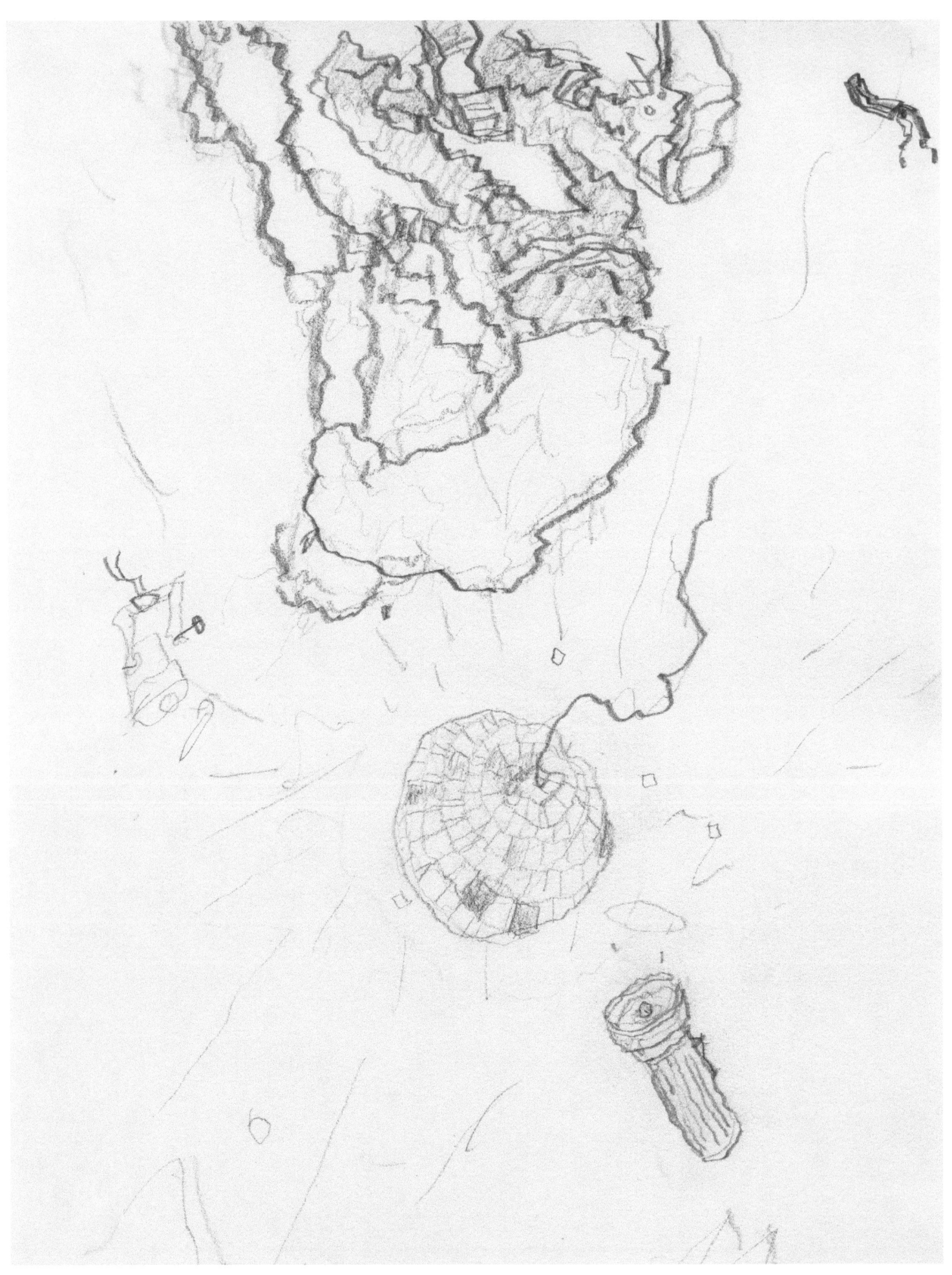

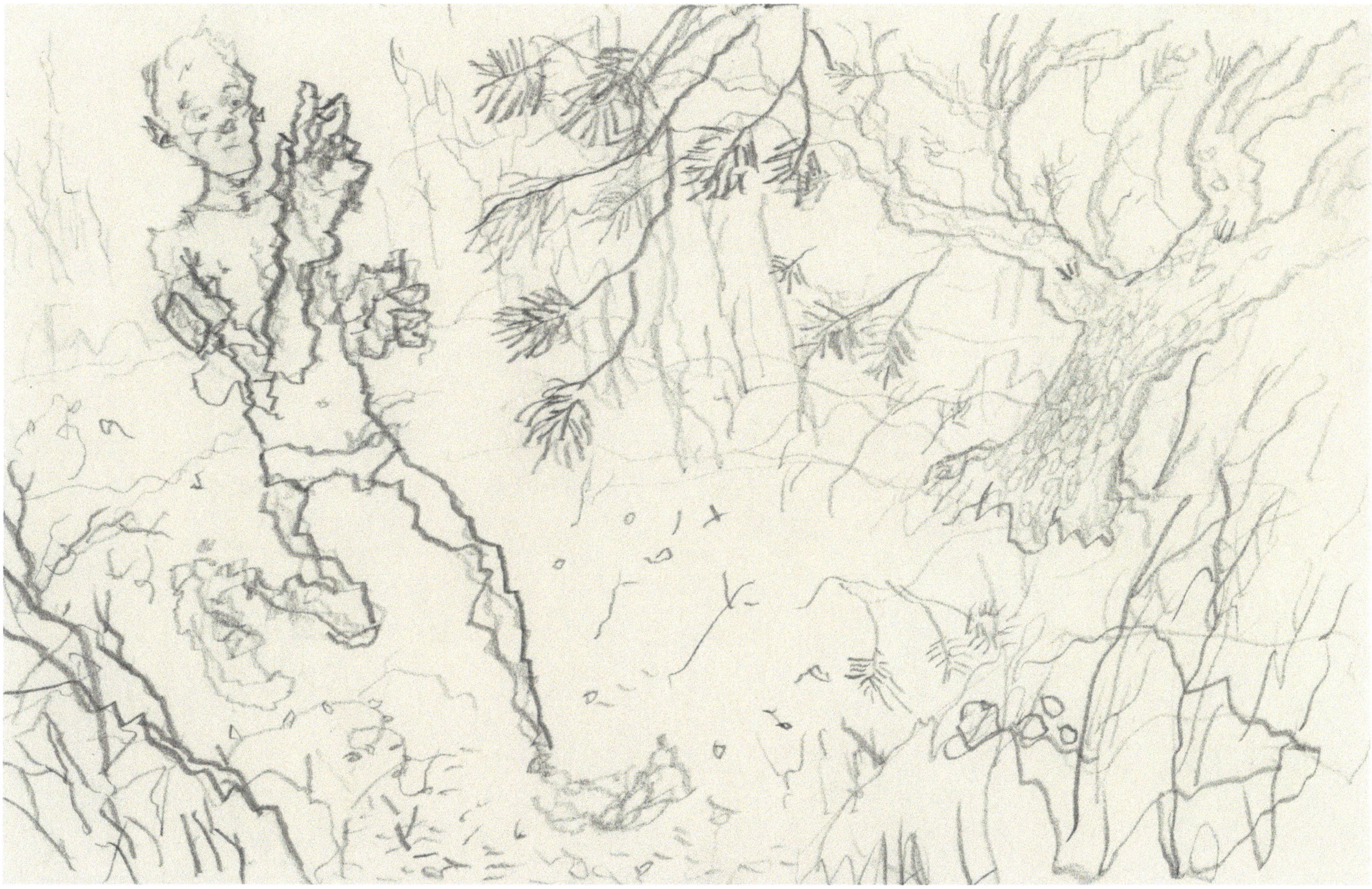

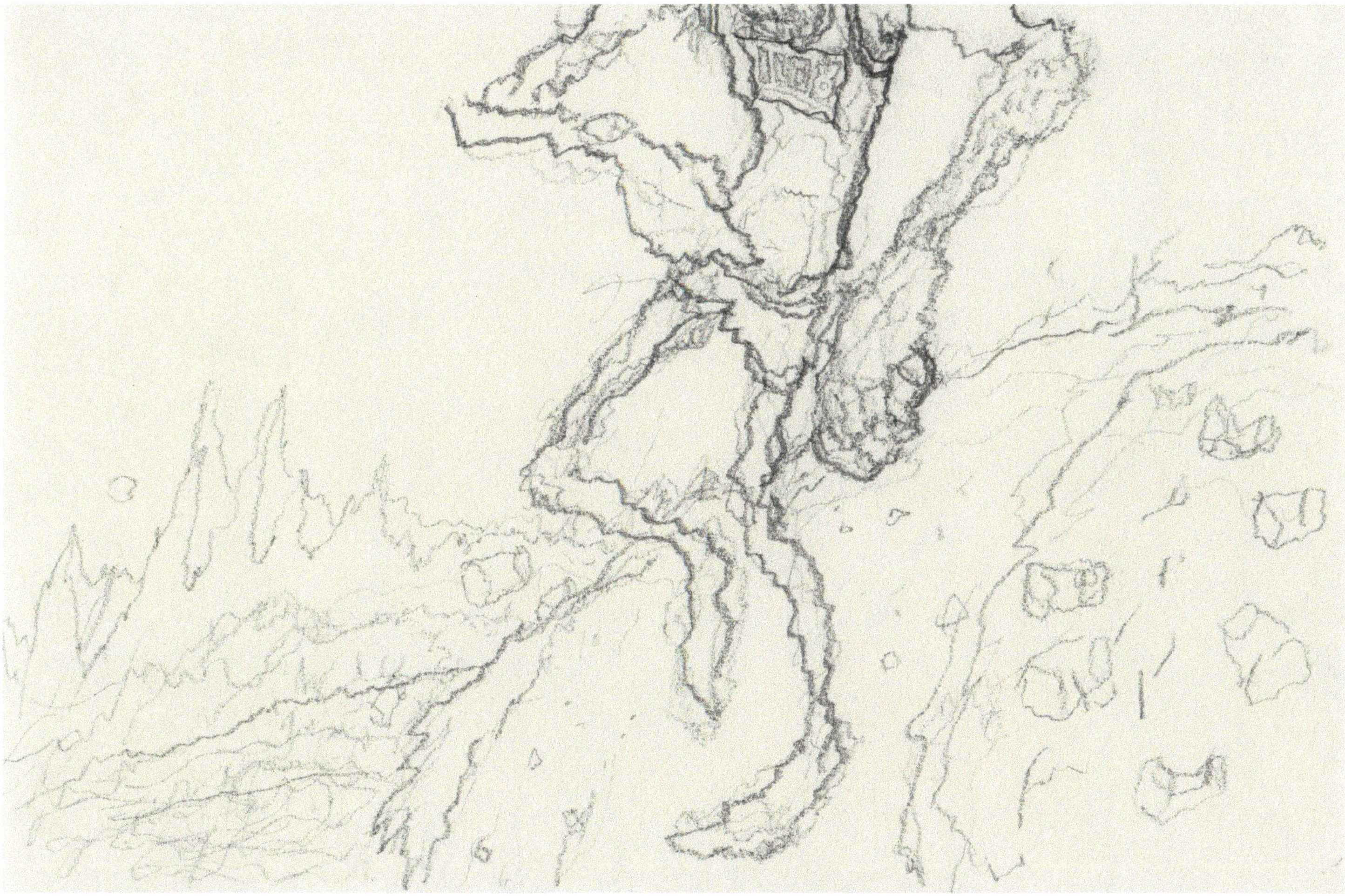

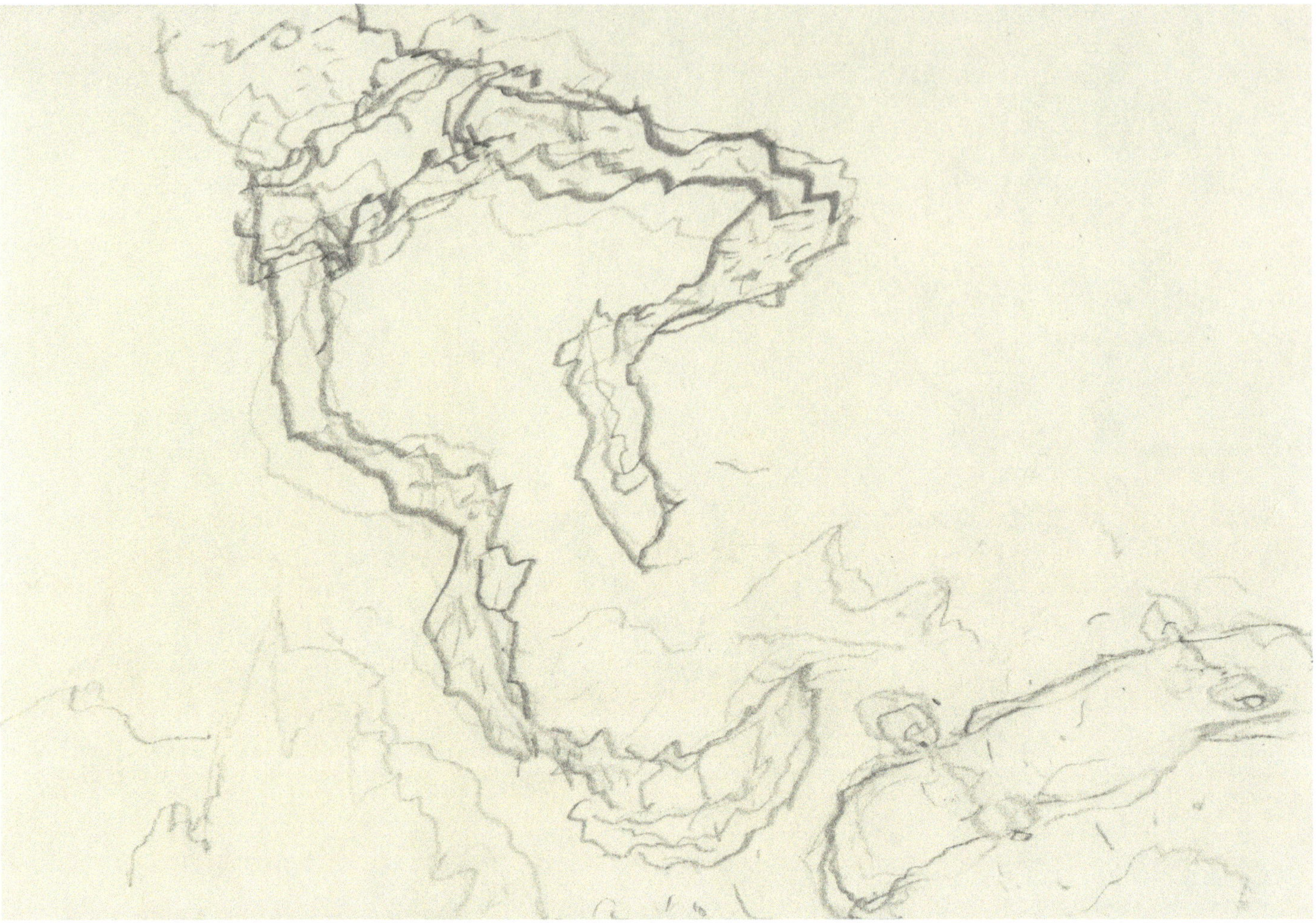

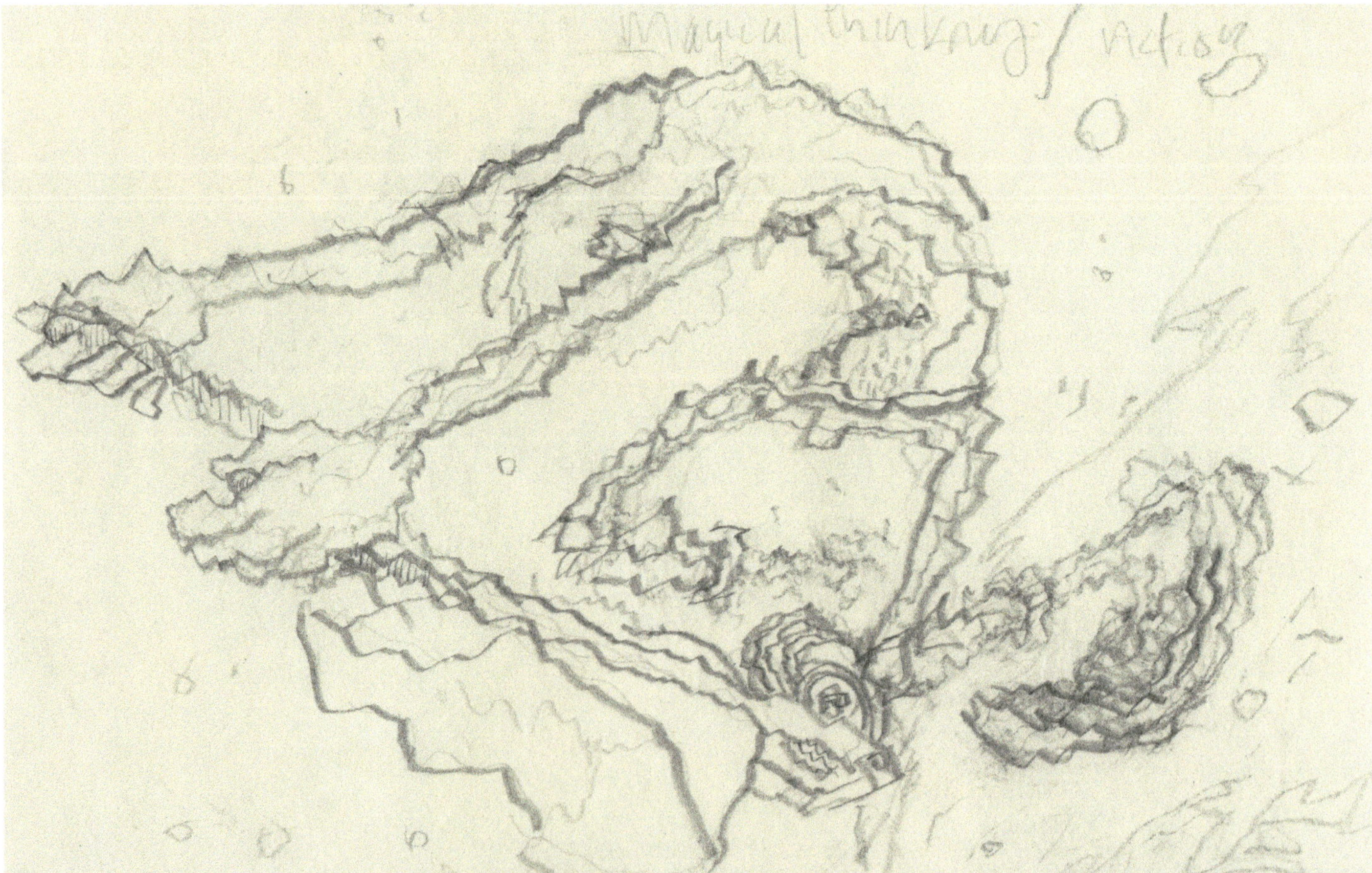

Magical thinking / Action

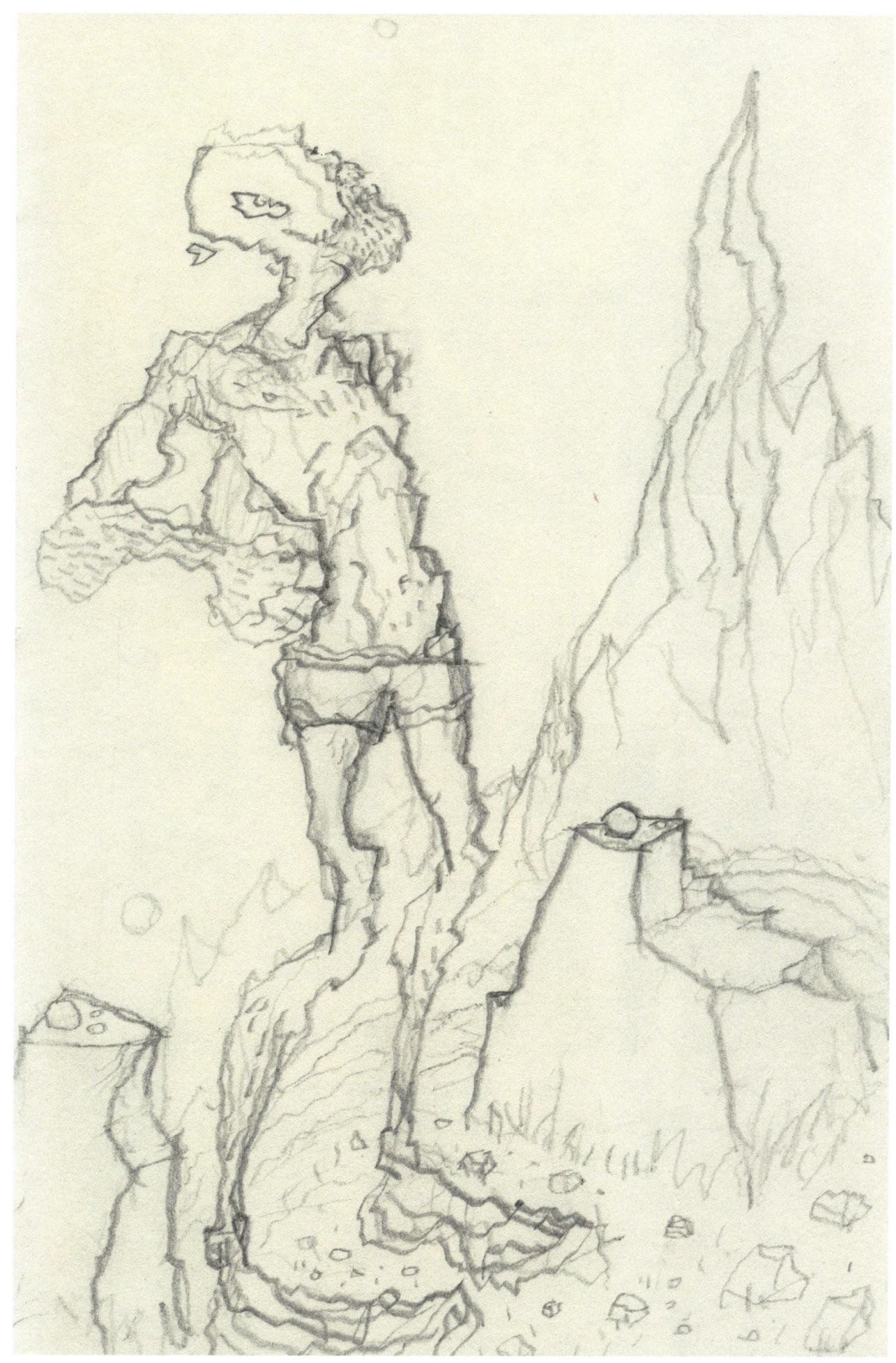

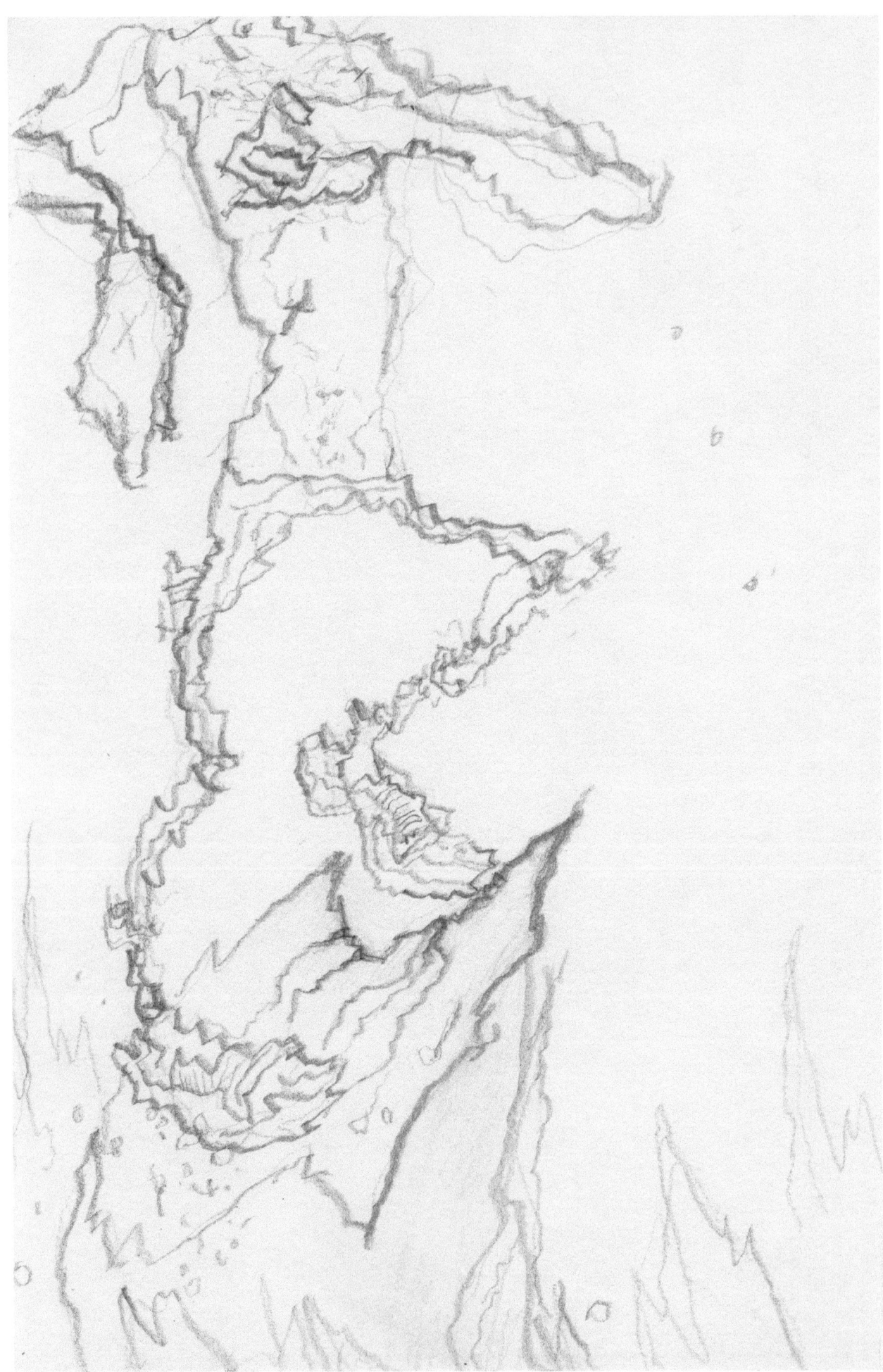

44

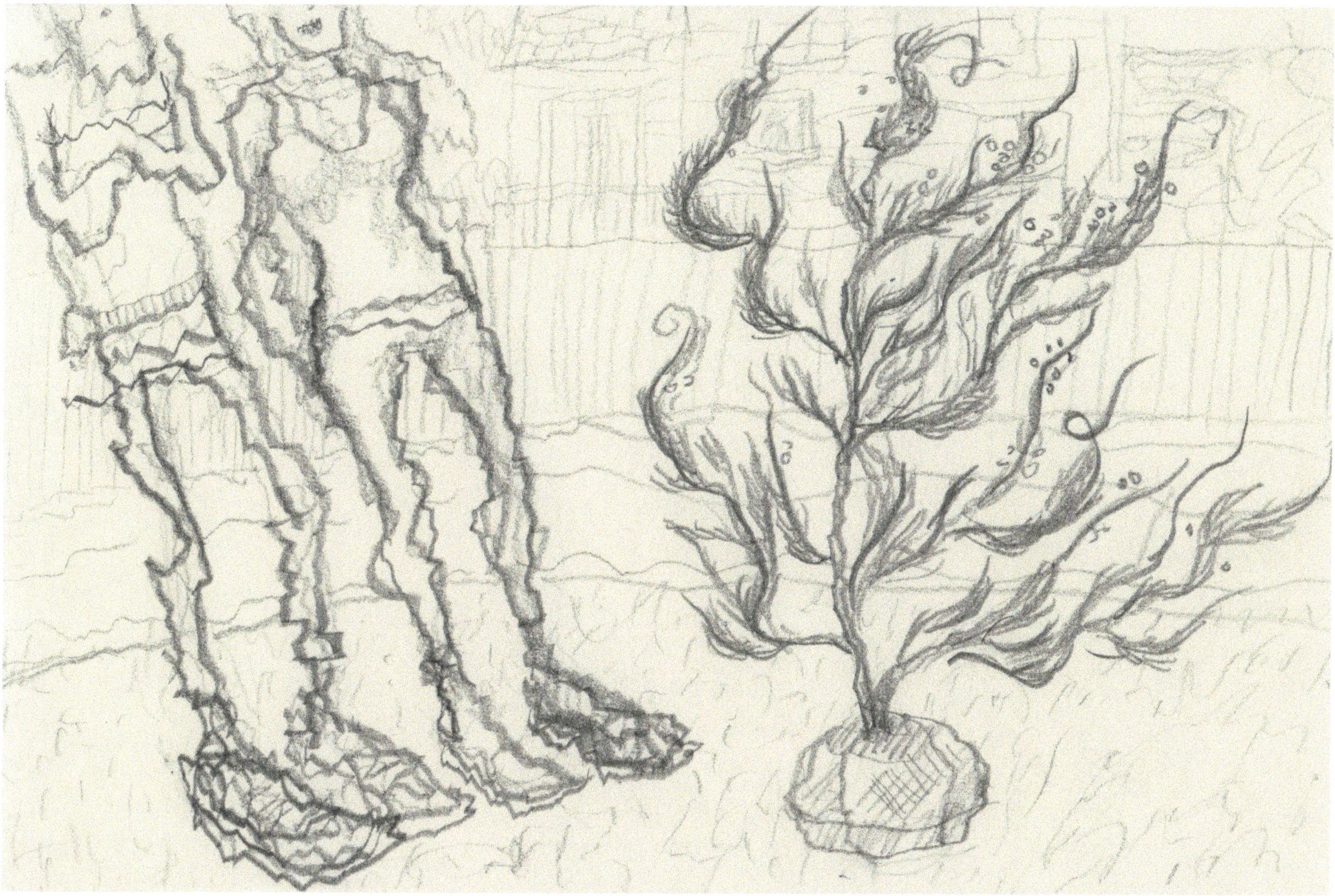

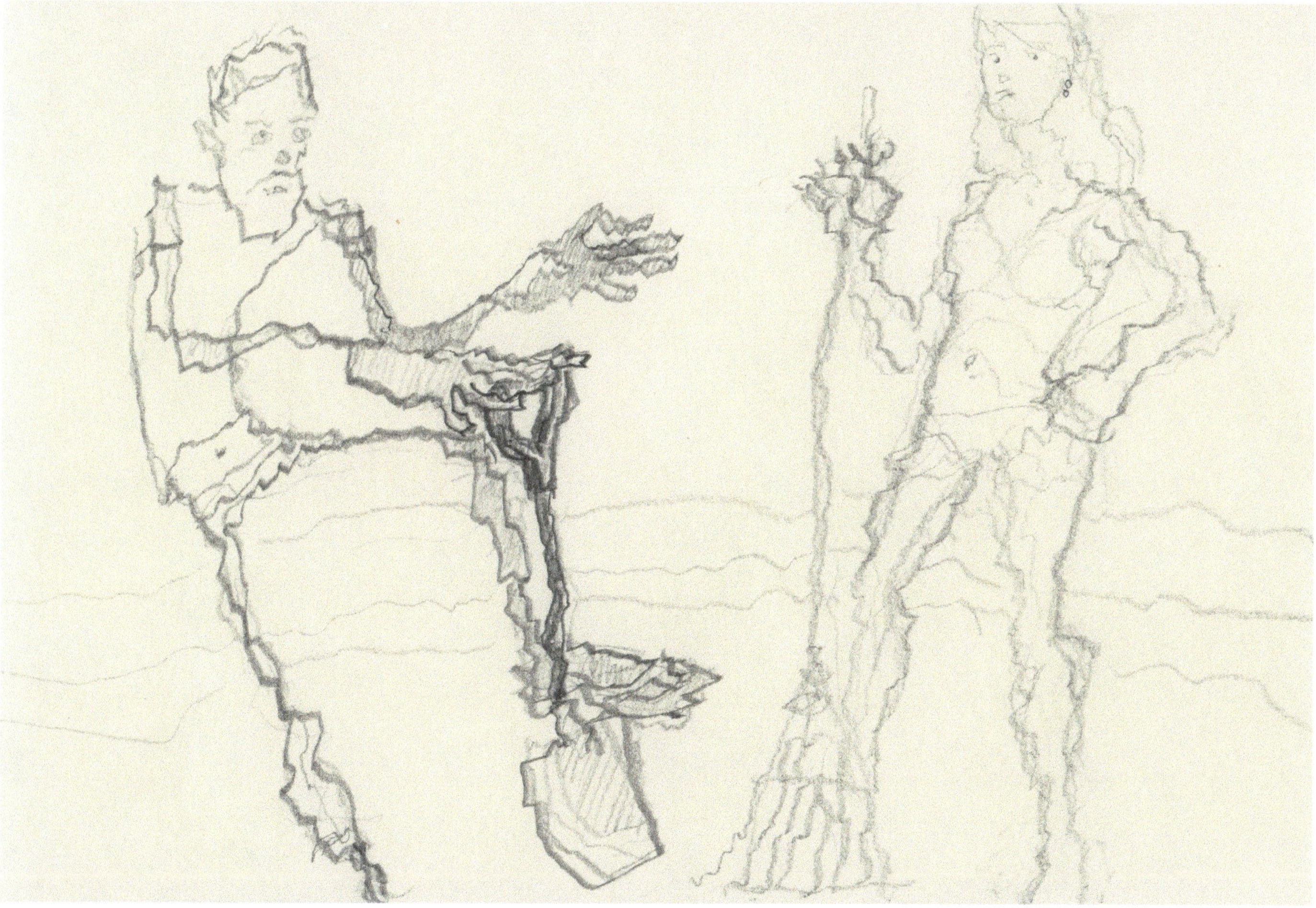

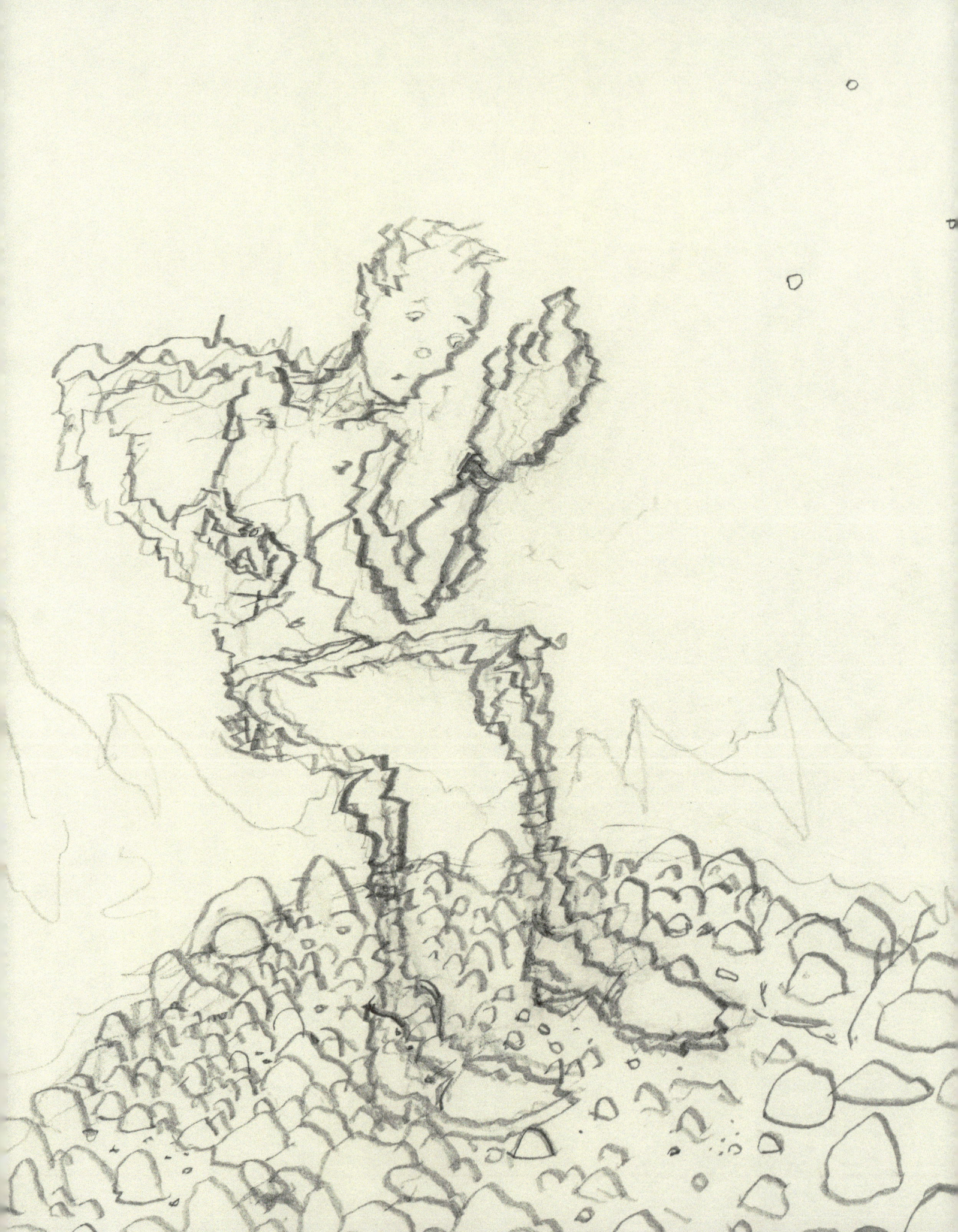

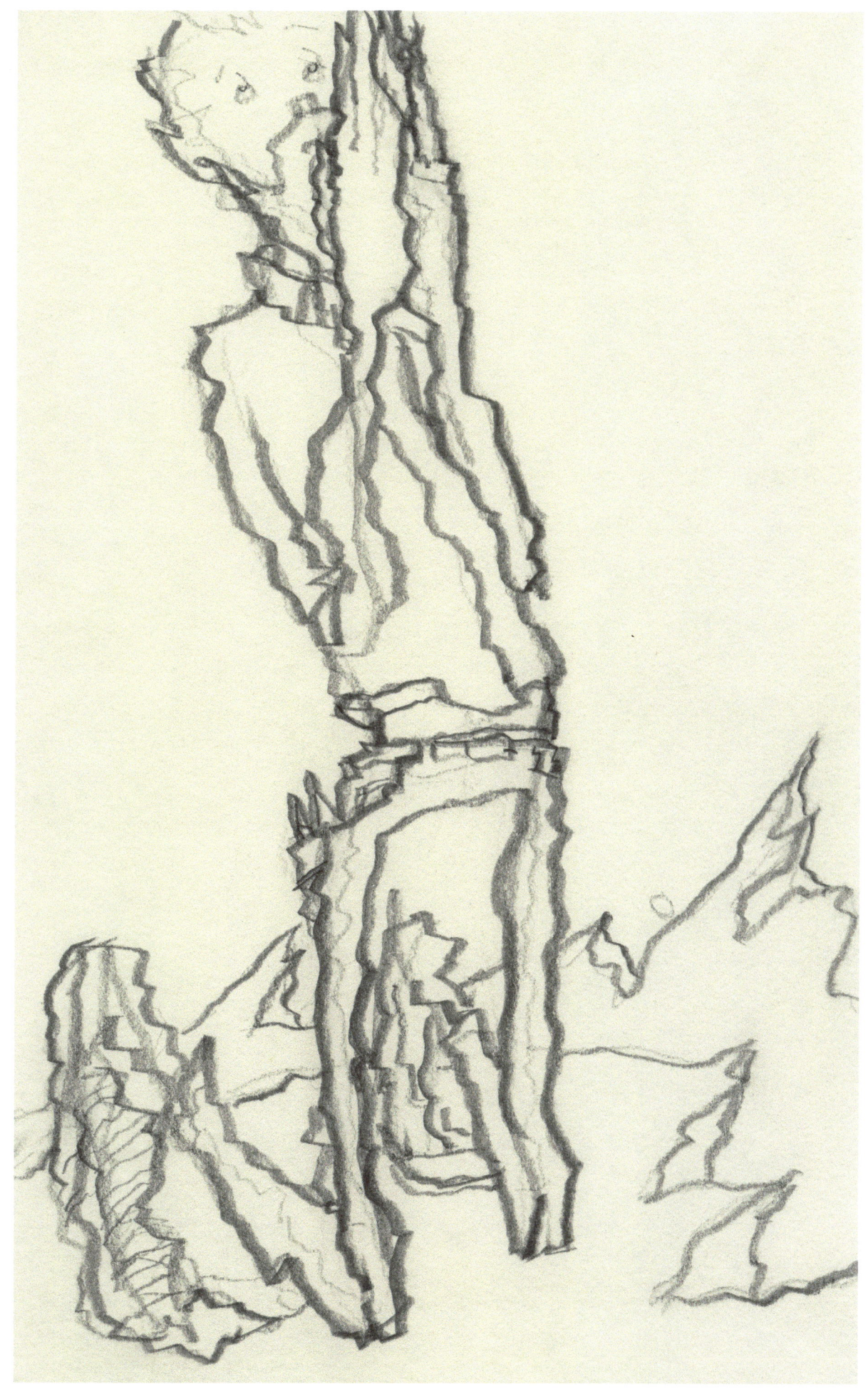

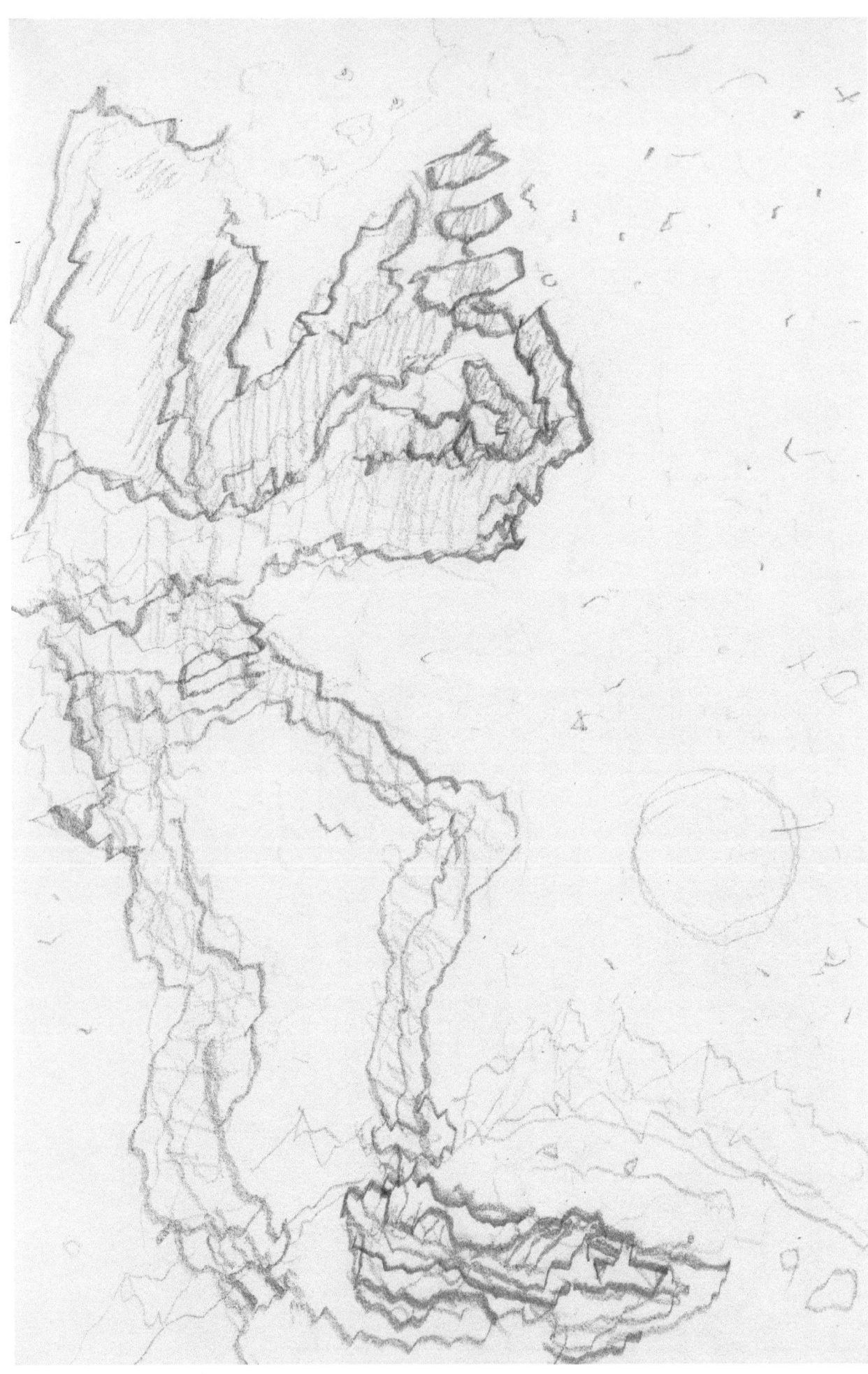

48

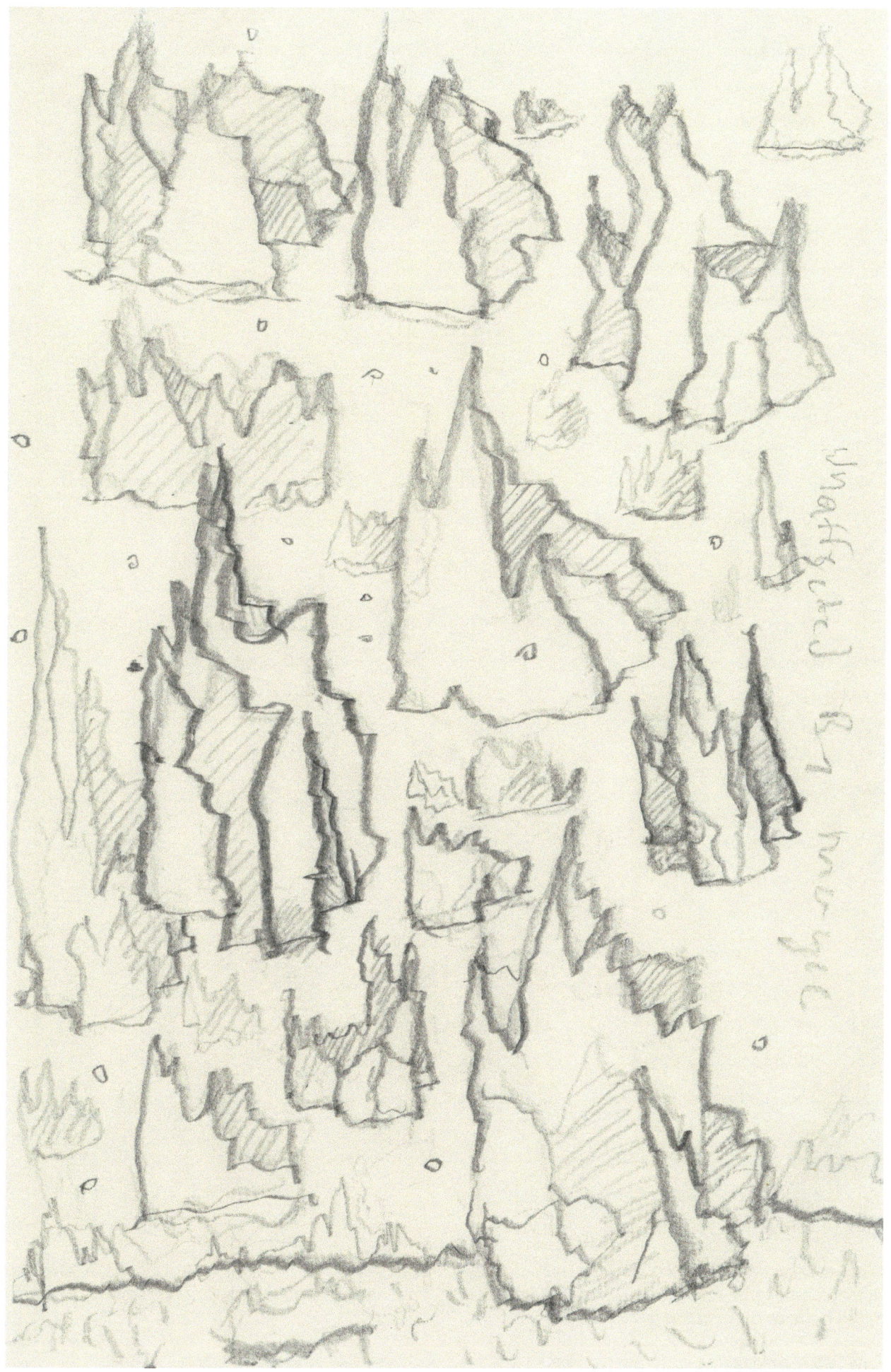

49

Copyright 2016 by Michael Nelson

ISBN-10: 0692821791
ISBN-13: 978-0692821794 (Cygnet Committee)

All rights reserved. This book may not be reproduced, in whole or in part, including illustrations, in any form (beyond that copying permitted by Section 107 and 108 of the U.S. Copyright Law and except by reviewers for the public press), without written permission from the publishers.

More info at: michaelnelsondrawings.com

www.ingramcontent.com/pod-product-compliance
Lightning Source LLC
Chambersburg PA
CBHW050901180526
45159CB00007B/2750